EDIBLE HEIRLOOMS

*heritage vegetables for
the maritime garden*

BILL THORNESS

SKIPSTONE

Published by Skipstone, an imprint of The Mountaineers Books
Manufactured in China

First printing 2009
12 11 10 09   5 4 3 2 1

Copy Editor: Alice Copp Smith
Design: Jane Jeszeck/Jigsaw, www.jigsawseattle.com
Cover photograph: *Pea pods* © Corbis
Back cover photograph: *January King* © Bill Thorness
Illustrator: Susie Thorness

Library of Congress Cataloging-in-Publication Data
Thorness, Bill, 1960-
Edible heirlooms : heritage vegetables for the maritime garden / by Bill Thorness.
   p. cm.
Includes bibliographical references and index.
ISBN 978-1-59485-142-1
1. Vegetables—Heirloom varieties—Washington (State)—Pacific Coast. 2.
Vegetables—Heirloom varieties—Oregon—Pacific Coast. I. Title.
SB324.73.T46 2009
635.09797—dc22

                              2009017766

Skipstone books may be purchased for corporate, educational, or other
promotional sales. For special discounts and information, contact our
Sales Department at 800-553-4453 or mbooks@mountaineersbooks.org.

Printed on recycled paper

Skipstone
1001 SW Klickitat Way
Suite 201
Seattle, Washington 98134
206-223-6303
www.skipstonepress.org
www.mountaineersbooks.org

LIVE LIFE. MAKE RIPPLES.

TABLE OF CONTENTS

Acknowledgments

My greatest thanks go to a number of people who helped me plan and research this book. They include garden educator Carl Elliott, David Cavagnaro of Seed Savers Exchange, Peggy Cornett of the Center for Historic Plants at Monticello, Josh Kirschenbaum and Tom Johns of Territorial Seed Co., Matthew Dillon at Organic Seed Alliance, and organic farmer and educator Michael Ableman. Thanks to Skipstone Press acquisitions editor Dana Youlin, and to the wise, good-humored copy editor Alice Copp Smith.

The support and first-reader task graciously offered by my wife, Susie Thorness, has helped me immensely, and it has been very gratifying to collaborate with her as the artist for this book.

The readings of many authors have influenced my work, but most particularly the works of the Kentucky farmer and philosopher Wendell Berry and the inquisitive gardener and omnivore Michael Pollan. More specifically, I have learned much from the garden writing of William Woys Weaver, Amy Goldman, Benjamin Watson, and Rosalind Creasy.

To augment my own research, I appreciate the efforts of my good friend Sylvia Kantor. Also, I am thankful for the librarians and wonderful book collection at the Elisabeth C. Miller Horticultural Library at the University of Washington's Center for Urban Horticulture, which will get all my gardening books when I finally return to the Earth to become compost.

But this book is not just a product of my interest in heirlooms and recent research. It also stems from my gardening education, which I realized when writing has long been directed toward heirlooms and seed saving as well as low-input, organic gardening practices. Along with the perennial guidance of Seattle Tilth's "Maritime Northwest Garden Guide," the writings of John Jeavons, Binda Colebrook, William Head, and, especially, Steve Solomon have been invaluable. For two decades of learning, I want especially to thank the current and past educators at Seattle Tilth, and commend their services to anyone in the Puget Sound area who wants to learn to grow their own food.

Finally, I would like to dedicate this book to my late father, Erick G. Thorness, who was a farmer, and to my extended family, which includes many who worked the land.

There is a moment after I sprinkle seeds onto the surface of my garden soil, before covering them up, when they blend with the soil and mineral particles and nearly disappear. An individual seed is so tiny—the pale, flat carrot seed, or the rough, rotund beet seed—that I think "There's no way this will feed me." But there it is, the beginning.

It's one time when I really drop down to ground level and get my eyes close to the garden soil. I scatter compost over the row of seeds and press it down with the edge of my palm, compacting the soil to snug the seeds into it. I picture each seed pulling moisture from the surrounding earth as it begins the process of sprouting to life.

Gardening is a contact sport for people as well as seeds—plunge in and get your hands dirty. Muddy knees, backaches, and grimy nails are all part of the game, along with sowing, weeding, mulching, and, of course, harvesting. Tamping down the row of seeds is the civilized method—gardeners used to stomp on the bed after planting, daring the seed to sprout, dancing for it.

I come from a farming family, and my earliest memories involve dirt, bare feet in garden rows, and hollyhock flower stalks towering over my head. But rarely as a boy did I consider the how and why of growing food or, frankly, take much interest in the kinds of plants being grown. It was simply the farm and the garden, and things just grew.

Becoming a gardener, as an adult, has been a journey of discovery, one that I expect will continue as long as I practice it. Learning the best techniques—tried-and-true ways that will yield consistent results—has been an essential part of my education. Before I migrated from the hot, dry plains of North Dakota to the verdant, temperate Pacific Northwest, my climate experience had consisted of beginning each year with blizzards and temperatures 40 degrees below Fahrenheit, which after a quick, muddy spring gave way to a hot summer of 100-degree days and the occasional rain that showed up in terrific thunderstorms.

What a difference to experience "Cascadia," the ever-green landscape seemingly defined by water, whether it be the rivers, lakes, ocean, or omnipresent rain. My grandmother, who had moved to "the Coast" when I was still a kid, would tell my mother in their regular phone calls about the Port Angeles grass that was green all winter, or the tulips that were in full bloom while I was still shoveling snow.

Once I arrived in Seattle, I was amazed by the fervor of growth. With such abundant natural beauty, being a gardener seemed almost required. And becoming a gardener, however challenging through inevitable mistakes along the way, seemed so much simpler in a place where things will just grow!

Almost from the first, I was attracted to heirloom vegetables. Twenty years ago I didn't think of them as such, but I was inspired by the idea of an old variety being kept alive from year to year as seed is passed from one generation to the next. Now some of these seeds grow in my garden—producing the same plant with the same-sized fruit in the same number of days as they did for Thomas Jefferson, or Native Americans, or settlers, or perhaps even my ancestors when they inhabited the Old Country.

The stories that come with these treasured seeds—a variety that was the favorite of royalty, a variety whose seeds were used as voting tokens by ancient peoples, a cultivar that was so popular it paid off the family mortgage—further spur the imagination. What kind of trellis did Jefferson build for his tall Alderman pea vines, and how did the Colville Indians cook with their Inchelium Red garlic? Stepping into my heirloom garden is not simply an education about how things grow, or a culinary expedition to see what's for dinner. It's like a living lesson on human history and the nature of civilization.

One of the greatest principles I've learned is to plan my garden with one eye on the future and keep the other eye on the past. What I've learned about biodiversity and ecological systems affects my understanding of nature and my impact on it. A desire to learn from the past has also directed me back toward heirloom plants.

I've learned that part of gardening with heirlooms is sharing in the collective wisdom. With that in mind, I began to research this book. *Edible Heirlooms* is focused on the growing conditions of the Pacific Northwest's maritime climate, found in coastal areas from San Francisco to Vancouver, British Columbia, from the base of mountain foothills to the Pacific Ocean. The book is a collection of more than two dozen vegetables for which heirloom varieties are available. It is not an exhaustive plant list, and you may grow heirloom varieties or plants not in this book. Perennial vegetables were not included, for example, and a few vegetables were omitted due to space constraints, lower popularity, or lack of good short-season heirloom choices. But in these pages you'll find information on many commonly available heirloom varieties that grow well in a cool, shorter-summer northern climate, and tips on how to grow them in our unique weather conditions. And on the book's accompanying website, www.edibleheirlooms.com, the exploration of heirloom vegetables will continue.

There is one lesson all gardeners can agree on, a mantra that has been part of the practice since raising your own food was the only way to survive and was as important as raising your children. From the beginning of soil cultivation to today, as predictably as the changing of the seasons, gardeners have always known this one thing: Keep growing.

What are heirlooms? It may come as no surprise that the question is debated regularly by gardeners who grow them or experts who oversee the process of keeping old varieties alive. An heirloom means different things to different people.

My definition starts with a sense of history. An heirloom plant has many differences from, and a few similarities to, a piece of antique furniture or a genealogy. Heirloom plants have histories that are shared by people passing them down. They originated in another era, and survived into this one. They chart our past and thereby help us make sense of the present. If my parents had not been married, and my great-grandparents had not immigrated, I would not be an American living right now. If old-country furniture had not been preserved and passed down, we would not have examples of how things were built and how people lived in the old days.

Unlike an antique table, an heirloom seed is alive, and in that way it is similar to me, as a product of my ancestors. But the Dinosaur kale seed contains a living memory, a genetic identity that would be the same as the Dinosaur kale grown 150 years ago in Tuscany. The old Italian farmer snapped off the knobby, blade-shaped leaves and chopped them into the soup, and I break off identical leaves for mine.

Because a seed is a living thing, it must be nurtured over many generations, lest the line die out. Humans produce a new generation every twenty or so years, but vegetables do not have that luxury. The life of an individual seed might be as little as one year or as many as ten, although a seed-saver would not keep a precious heirloom that long without regrowing it and gaining new seed. To remain fresh and vigorous, heirloom seeds must be "grown out" at least every five years. To keep the seed stock healthy, then, requires a great deal of effort by many people. Organizations such as Seed Savers Exchange (SSE) and Southern Exposure Seed Exchange are indispensable: not only do they grow and save seed (and they're getting more sophisticated about it all the time), but they also serve as a nexus for a community of seed-savers who participate in this vital process. A few seed companies also participate in this process. But in order for seed diversity and heirloom plants to live on, you and I and other gardeners must take part too.

To me, the fact that home gardeners grow and save and pass on its seed is also a characteristic of a true heirloom. Some old varieties have become so popular that they are widely available commercially, but the plants to truly cherish as heirlooms are the ones you won't find in every seed catalog or in 4-inch pots on the tables at your local nursery. Many popular vegetable cultivars have been created through hybridization to achieve commercially desirable traits such as shelf stability or shipping hardiness. The thin-skinned tomato that bruises if handled three times would not survive the supermarket, but it very well might be the most delectable fruit on the dinner table.

My definition of an heirloom includes four requirements. First, it has been grown by previous generations since at least before World War II, after which commercial hybridization and long-distance produce shipping really took off. Second, the cultivar is not in broad commercial distribution today. Third, it is open-pollinated, which means that the seed is produced by natural, random pollination, rather than by controlled methods, as is done to create hybrids. Finally, for inclusion in the book, I chose plants for which seed is still regularly available, either through bio-regional seed companies or through seed-saving organizations. Even so, because some plants yield only small quantities of seed, they may periodically disappear from your favorite seed suppliers' catalogs. Keep searching; they're worth the effort.

Many people rave about advancements in plant breeding that have given us higher yields, earlier ripening, and more resistance to pests and diseases. I agree that hybrids certainly have their place, and I don't hesitate to grow hybrids when appropriate. In some years, maritime gardeners would not have ripe tomatoes to put on their table if it weren't for the short-season varieties bred to produce tomatoes even in Alaska. And I have occasionally grown a hybrid that is so flavorful as to command a spot in the garden—it was just that good.

But I grow heirlooms whenever possible, for several reasons.

First, I am concerned about biodiversity, a term that was taking hold in conservation circles about the time I was digging my first maritime garden. Short for "biological diversity," the term was popularized in the late 1980s by biologist and writer Edward O. Wilson as suggesting a holistic approach to ecosystems, one that recognizes value in variation. We may not understand the interplay among all of nature's diverse species, but we do know that loss of diversity is a one-way road, irreversible and catastrophic.

WHY GROW HEIRLOOMS?

What biodiversity implies to me, as a home gardener, is this: because my landscape is an ecosystem, it deserves respect and nurture. If I cleared out all the plants that attract pollinating insects or that contribute nutrients to the soil, my ecosystem would be poorer (and my gardening would suffer). The challenge for me is to somehow integrate my vegetable-growing practices into a diverse ecosystem and, if possible, enhance biodiversity. I do that by nurturing unique cultivars that may have very different traits from what my neighbors are growing.

Sadly, agricultural practices in the United States in the 20th and 21st centuries have gone in the other direction. In his book *Earth in the Balance,* Al Gore writes, "of all the varieties of vegetables listed the Department of Agriculture in 1900, no more than 3 percent now remain." Since the 1940s, large-scale farming has promoted monoculture and genetic uniformity over diversity. I believe we must protect what little food crop biodiversity still exists. The alternative could be further food crises, or cataclysmic events on the scale of the Irish potato famine or the American corn crop collapse in the 1970s.

In Ireland in the 1840s, peasants relied on the variety of potato known as the "lumper" as their primary food source. Potato blight destroyed nearly all of the crop in 1845, and then flared up again in 1846 to destroy the remaining seed crop shortly after it had been planted. Starvation ensued in part because the populace was so dependent upon the lumper as the food they could afford.

Such problems are not lost to the dim past. In fact, today we may be in even more danger of massive crop failures that could have far-reaching effects. In 1970, a fungus called southern corn leaf blight swept across America's genetically similar corn crop in four months, causing trading panic, emergency actions by the U.S. government and seed suppliers, and commodity price spikes.

A 15 percent loss in the country's corn crop was caused by a genetic alteration, bred into most hybrid corn seed, that provided a "window" in the seed through which the fungus could pass. Although corrective action limited widespread crop loss to one year, the blight could have easily impacted most segments of the American food system, from meat production to foreign trade. And if suspicion about whether the blight might harm humans eating that corn had taken hold (like the regular "tainted produce" scares we are seeing today), the damage could have multiplied faster than the blight itself.

The second reason I grow heirlooms is that I want to vote with my pocketbook. When I buy seeds, I want to support biodiversity and the people doing that work. The loss of diversity in our seed companies has paralleled the loss of varieties. The sixth edition of the *Garden Seed Inventory* published by Seed Savers Exchange in 2004 noted that "57 percent of the nearly 5,000 non-hybrid vegetable varieties offered in 1984 catalogs had been dropped by 2004." It blamed buyouts and mergers in the garden-seed industry and the focus on hybrids, and said the worst loss occurred between 1984 and 1987, when nearly one-quarter of U.S. and Canadian mail-order seed companies (fifty-four out of 230) went out of business or were acquired by larger companies.

However, renewed concern and interest (and tireless work by SSE and like-minded people) showed a bright spot in the diversity battle. The 2004 *Inventory* (a publication produced only every few years) also noted that "2,559 entirely new varieties have been introduced just during the last six years!" That number included some heirloom varieties that were being reintroduced by seed companies along with the new varieties. But availability is still unreliable: about half of the 8,494 commercially available seeds in the *Inventory* were listed as being offered by only one source.

It's clear that our vegetable heritage is on shaky ground. We cannot afford to take our attention away from the loss of diversity, and seed-savers' organizations cannot do the work alone. To ensure that no more beloved old varieties disappear, gardeners must show commercial seed companies that they value heirlooms by buying them. Right now, some of the most active seed-saving individuals have created cottage industries growing heirloom seed for small seed houses, and this is a vital part of the heirloom preservation movement.

The next advancement in this movement is for produce from heirloom seeds and plants to be grown and sold to the public. In the last ten years, the country has seen a boom in small farming on a scale that is amazing and viable. Market gardens and small local farms have grown up around urban and suburban areas. Their fresh, often organic produce is trucked in daily to farmers markets and, increasingly, to the produce departments of large grocery stores. To differentiate their offerings from produce grown in a hothouse, or shipped in from perennially warm climates half a world away, these local farmers need a unique product, and many times the answer is heirlooms.

Home gardeners are far more numerous than farmers, and by supporting the growing of heirloom varieties, we can effectively make the cornucopia of varieties available again commercially. Imagine a unique tomato variety that five years ago could only be found in the form of seed from Seed Savers Exchange showing up as ripe produce in the bins at your local Sunday market—delightful! By voting with our pocketbooks—both when we buy seed and when we choose to buy from local farmers (and especially their heirloom crops)—we will be magnifying the effect of our purchases.

Along with these reasons to grow heirlooms, I grow them for their stories. Before the introduction of the printing press, oral tradition was the essential way to preserve and transfer cultural lore. As we grow heirlooms and share seeds, plants, and produce, we have the opportunity to keep that tradition alive. Just as an antique has more value if its provenance is known, so too does an heirloom vegetable or fruit bring more delight when it's accompanied by its origin story. Such a story is a delightful discovery for the listener and a satisfying closing of the loop for the deliverer. As you perpetuate a plant, do the same with its lore.

THE PURE FOOD REVOLUTION

The organic and local food revolutions of recent years have taught the American shopper a lesson that sustainable gardeners and market farmers have long known: fresh, pure food is better. Fruit and vegetables untainted by chemical fertilizers have won taste tests, and scientific studies have proven them to be more nutritious as well.

To me, sustainable gardening means growing my food with as little external input as possible. I'll gladly pull weeds by hand rather than use herbicides. As much as possible, I want to make and use my own compost from a compost pile and from the worm bin that recycles my kitchen scraps. If my garden soil needs more nutrition, I'll add the most basic purchased fertilizer, manure, and compost, but I always choose a certified organic product whose label reveals all of its ingredients. I seek certified organic seed, and every year I'm saving more seed to regrow my own.

When I garden organically, I know that I not only produce the purest fresh food for my table but also avoid contributing harmful chemicals to the environment. Chemicals never waft through the air to my neighbors' properties, or leach into the groundwater under my home and end up in public waterways. It's the least I can do to respect the natural world that enables me to live a healthy life, and to honor the many gifts that I receive as a gardener.

BECOMING A LOCAL FOOD ACTIVIST

Recently I discovered a name for my condition. It's something that caused an itch I needed to scratch, an affliction for which I tried many possible treatments. I grew my own medications. I sought out area shamans and brought home their prescriptions. I joined communities of others who share my condition. Finally, it was given a name. With that, I realized how many more people not only had it too but were seeking the same remedies. In 2007 it became clear: I am a locavore.

It seems so obvious now. All that searching for the freshest local food from farmers and trading with other amateur growers. The sowing, the nurturing, the reaping—you'd think that would be enough, but then there would just be more sowing.

On a more serious note, this enlightenment was more than just a personal realization—it was an affirmation of something I have been supporting and working toward for many years. Many more people are embracing the idea that whenever possible, food should be a fresh, local experience. The locavore movement is encouraging people to garden, yes, but also to pay attention to where their food comes from, by what means it is grown, and when it was harvested, and how it is brought to market. I am proud to be part of the social network that has participated in raising this awareness. It is a natural outgrowth of being a gardener.

It is locavores (whether or not we embrace that title) who are helping bring into existence a new generation of farmers, one that is practicing an old-is-new style of farming. Together, farmers and supporters are preserving valuable farmland near cities, stemming the suburban sprawl that used to seem inevitable, and bringing the idea of local produce back into the public consciousness. More people are realizing that we can buy fresh, local produce rather than just the mass-transported, prepackaged supermarket version, and the recognition often comes with the idea that we can—and possibly should—break ground for our own little patch of favorite veggies.

This realization is important for the preservation of heirlooms because it is also a recognition of variety, flavor, and uniqueness. All broccoli does not have to be large, green heads, and all tomatoes don't need to be perfectly round, 3-inch globes. Variety is the first spice to be used when you are creating a delightful stew. Embracing the opportunity to try a dozen different heirloom cultivars of our favorite vegetables supports the source of that diversity and ensures its continuance.

Simply by virtue of being gardeners, we are part of a locavore community. It doesn't get more local than bringing produce in from the backyard—food that travels 50 feet rather than the national average distance of 1,500 miles is quite a revolution.

We can take the concept one step further and save seed from our heirloom plants. People who generate their own electricity through solar power speak of being "off the grid," meaning that they don't have to tap into the commercial energy system.

Gardeners can achieve a similar goal, by closing the loop on our growing practices with the small act of saving seed. Couple it with making compost and we will move even closer to a self-sustaining system. We can create links to others in this alternative grid by sharing seeds with friends or with a seed-savers' organization.

Being a locavore presents grass-roots opportunities to create community too. People of like mind can bring farmers markets to their neighborhoods. They can turn vacant lots and unused public land into community gardens for use by people who don't have their own land. Gardeners are a valuable resource for food banks, especially when we band together and create "giving gardens" that can deliver hundreds or even thousands of pounds of fresh food each year to neighbors in need. More local food dollars strengthen the economy. Through financial and volunteer efforts, locavores also can support an infrastructure of educational and activist nonprofit organizations dedicated to building local food systems. Being involved in these efforts boosts community pride and strengthens residents' sense of place.

By working toward a more locally focused society, gardeners can have a much greater impact than simply growing our own food. What we don't grow, we can make an effort to buy from local farmers, reducing our "carbon footprints" and easing environmental stress on the local ecosystem. Keeping our food dollars in our communities helps create local economies that can support the availability of local produce, and the system will—pardon the expression—feed on itself and grow. Once our efforts reach the scale of commercial viability, new opportunities can arise, such as feeding schoolchildren with produce from local farmers.

To become a locavore, you can start by simply picking up a packet of heirloom seeds. Where each of us takes it from there is a matter of time, energy, and imagination.

GROWING BIO-REGIONALLY

A great diversity of heirloom varieties is being cultivated and preserved around the world. However, what grows well in the mountains of Austria or in the deserts of New Mexico may not do well in a cool coastal region. Along with choosing varieties that are particularly suited to a maritime climate, an heirloom gardener can get a growing advantage by buying from a seed company that grows its seed in maritime conditions, or by exchanging seed with a seed-saving friend in the same region. This is the bio-regional approach.

A bio-regional seed company also tries to grow its plants in the climate where its customers live. Although not many do this, partly because of industry consolidation and partly because the available quantity of regionally grown seed may not be consistent from one year to the next, seed companies that are committed to bio-regional growing often cite this benefit in their literature.

Territorial Seed Company, based in Cottage Grove, Oregon, is a bio-regional seed provider. Owner Tom Johns told me that even though the popular heirloom tomato Brandywine is certainly not the shortest-season tomato on his list, maritime gardeners find his Brandywine seed grows better in the maritime climate than seed from other suppliers. This is because for years his company has been growing and selecting the most vigorous, best-producing Brandywines and saving their seed. In other words, the Brandywine sold by Territorial has been bred for conditions in the maritime Northwest.

A bio-regional company is in the best position to know what the farmers and home gardeners of its region want and like. Being connected to the communities to which they sell, bio-regional seed companies also will be more sensitive about providing seeds of

plants that are culturally important to preserve. Some gardeners take this idea much further, and suggest that to preserve true cultural diversity gardeners grow only plants that originated or were developed in their region.

Some activists, such as Gary Paul Nabhan of New Mexico, are promoting native regional foods as part of the cultural heritage of a given area. A noted author and conservationist, Nabhan created the Renewing America's Food Traditions (RAFT) Alliance, which identifies endangered or threatened American regional foods and seeks to preserve them.

In addition to native varieties, many of our valued heirlooms are immigrants, their paths tracing those of our ancestors. So it is valuable for many reasons to understand a plant's place of origin and regional significance.

When you patronize bio-regional seed companies, you're buying local, which keeps your seed dollars close to home, and the produce you grow from those seeds lowers your carbon footprint. But you're also supporting a business that believes, as you do, in the importance of food crop diversity and regionality. As these seed sources become fewer, it is increasingly important to practice bio-regionalism.

SITE SELECTION, SEASON EXTENDERS, AND STRUCTURES

O ur maritime climate presents some unique food gardening challenges. We want to take best advantage of the sun, and we need to combat plant diseases that thrive in our moist environment. If we want to garden year-round, convenience and access during the rainy season are important.

These concerns can be addressed by proper siting of the garden on your property, planning how to extend the gardening season, and building structures to boost productivity or enhance the harvest.

Start small. Choose which of the ideas below interest you, and don't feel you need to implement everything in order to have a successful garden. You don't have to re-create the family farm. A garden of any size or scope is a success if you are enjoying it and using it.

Some gardeners are constrained by space, others by limited available time, and still others by the amount of physical effort they can put forth, but even if you have a scant amount of any of the three, you can still grow some wonderful heirloom vegetables. With a bit of forethought, your gardening can fit your interests and skills. Very little garden space? Mix Speckled Trout, Red Oak

Leaf, and Green Deer Tongue lettuce together in a windowbox, or enjoy the grey-green foliage and juicy red fruit of the Silvery Fir Tree tomato in a pot on the patio. Lots of space but little time? The Rouge Vif d'Etampes pumpkin will gloriously fill a bed and leave you free to watch the Cinderella story come to life. Not as able-bodied as you once were? Scale back to a border of colorful, nutritious Rainbow chard and sprinkle the rest of the garden with cover-crop seeds.

SITE SELECTION

Whatever the scale of your garden, choosing a proper site is an important first step. The maritime climate is typified by long, cool springs, and when the sun reaches its northernmost point in the year, our growing season is just getting going—most of our home-grown produce hasn't yet attained its maximum size or started to ripen. Therefore it's vital to maximize sun exposure, especially for heat-loving vegetables such as tomatoes and peppers, which need six hours of full sun per day to thrive. I've had best success with tomatoes when they're front-and-center in the sunniest spot in the yard, oriented to the south for overhead exposure and to the west for the warmest, late-afternoon rays. I never seem to have trouble finding shadier spots to grow the more tender vegetables, like salad greens, that need a little shade during our warmer weeks.

Consider what might be blocking sun from reaching your plants at different times of day. Trees or a hedge on the perimeter of the garden may be great windbreaks, but they can cast shade on your garden, especially during late-summer tomato-ripening time—when, unfortunately, the sun is tracking lower in the sky. Look also beyond the obvious shade culprits. Do you have quick-growing, tall perennials such as giant grasses, or have you installed trellises for vining veggies? You might have to move such plants or structures to maximize sun exposure.

If you just don't have a sun-drenched location, your solution for growing a prizewinning Jimmy Nardello's Italian Sweet pepper or a Cherokee Purple tomato might be a large pot that you can move periodically to track the sun.

Winter sun presents a different calculation. To capture the weaker rays on shorter days, the sunniest part of the garden may be the best place for hardy salad greens, and the prime location for a season extender like the plastic hoop house known as a cloche. I try to plan and plant my winter vegetables so I can put up a cloche that faces south and west. Putting greens into the sunny spot where I grew tomatoes also means I'm rotating crops, which increases soil fertility and helps prevent plant diseases.

Wind can be both a positive and a negative factor on your garden site. It will help dry out soil faster in spring so that you can get a jump on the planting season, but it also can create harsher conditions for gardening in fall and winter. If wind is a factor, site the garden on the south side of a gentle slope if possible, with a permeable windbreak like a hedge that is distant enough to not cause a shade problem. The windbreak also can make it easier to work with season-extending devices.

I also try to orient the beds so I have easy access during the rainy winter months. I want to pop out on a blustery afternoon to snip some salad greens or herbs without getting muddy, and to easily reach into a cloche or a cold frame from a path or the edge of a raised bed.

If much of your best garden space is already landscaped, you still may be able to work in some food crops. Heirloom vegetables are beautiful as well as delicious, and they can make attractive additions to a summer border or perennial bed. A row of Rossa di Treviso radicchio, with its elongated oval leaves tinged with a deep plum color, can complement a border bed of flowers, while the showy pink, red, and white blooms of the Painted Lady runner bean will blaze regally when trellised onto a fence behind low perennial shrubs.

SEASON EXTENDERS

In my year-round edible landscape, I am sometimes turning garden soil while the ski slopes are at their busiest. Later in the year I often have tomatoes still ripening while landlocked northerners are sending their children to school amid snow flurries. Such a long growing season is made possible by mild maritime temperatures, but the trade-off is a lack of sustained hot days during summer, so necessary for full ripening of warm-season crops, such as our beloved tomatoes.

Extending the season and artificially providing warmth to the garden become valuable techniques. I use a variety of season-extending tools, such as cold frames, cloches, floating row covers, or the "Wall O' Water."

A cold frame is a rigid, boxlike structure, usually made of glass or plastic attached to a wood frame. It is basically a small, portable greenhouse. The top is slanted to shed moisture and grab more sunlight. It doesn't have to be large or complex—a 3-foot-square box

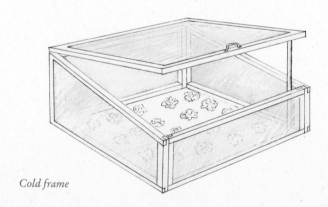

Cold frame

made of 2 x 2's and rigid plastic sheeting is ideal. An old window in its frame, propped up on artfully stacked bricks, can work well too. There are many great designs available that you can create at low cost.

A cold frame can house a lush bed of winter greens or carrots, or it can be used to warm the soil and get an early start on your Dwarf Grey Sugar peas. It can also cover a nursery bed for closely sown seedlings that you will separate and transplant after the weather warms. Or it can be a place where you can set potted seedlings to "harden off"—an intermediate step in their journey from being sprouted indoors to being planted out to face the spring elements. It is propped open when necessary, so as not to overheat the plants, and to allow watering.

A cloche is perhaps more portable than a cold frame, or at least more compact for storage. A common design, known as a hoop house, uses lengths of flexible polyvinylchloride (PVC) pipe bent into arcs, with each end fastened to the ground within a sleeve of larger pipe or slid over a piece of rebar. Two or more such hoops laid out in a row form a tunnel under which your plants will grow. The pipes are connected along the top and sides with crossbars

Hoop-house cloche

of plastic or bamboo, tied at each hoop to provide more rigidity. A clear plastic sheet is then stretched over the top and ends and secured on all sides to create a greenhouse effect. Garden supply companies sell plastic sleeves that clip onto the hoops to hold the sheeting in place. The plastic draped over the ends can be rolled up for watering and to allow air circulation, ensuring that the plants don't overheat on warmer days.

In the maritime garden, the cloche can be taken down when the weather warms, or it can be left in place and the plastic sheeting replaced with a spun-polyester fabric known as floating row cover. This material lets light, air, and moisture through, but its tightly woven mesh provides filtered shade, so a bed of cool-season greens might still thrive in a hot location.

Floating row cover also is used directly on the ground. It can cover an open garden bed prior to planting, to help warm the soil. It can keep out unwanted insects, such as the carrot rust fly, which is common in Northwest gardens. It also keeps slugs and snails off tender young plants and prevents birds from stealing your seed. It is effective against cabbage maggots and flea beetles as well. It can be left on some crops, such as carrots, all season, but taken off other crops, such as squash or cabbage, as the plants grow. It must be removed from any plant that is pollinated by insects as soon as flowering begins.

Wall O' Water is the brand name of a temporary, open-topped plastic cloche that maritime Northwest gardeners commonly use around young tomatoes or other heat-loving plants to give them an earlier start. It is a vertical ring of fused plastic tubes 18 inches tall and open on each end. This circular "wall" is placed vertically over a newly planted tomato or pepper, and the tubes are filled with water, which acts as an insulator. When it is mostly full, the tops of the tubes slump toward the center of the circle, thereby forming a teepee-shaped cloche over the plant. As the plant grows, the ring can be propped open with sticks plunged into the soil within the circle. This device has allowed me to plant tomatoes in my Seattle garden as early as the first weekend of May—a month before the recommended nighttime temperatures for tomatoes have been reached. Although some people leave the Wall O' Water around the plant until midsummer, I remove mine when temperatures are predictably warm and the tomato has grown out the top, has begun to vine, and needs to be tied to a support.

The Wall O' Water is an updated version of an old-time cloche shaped like a bell. The bell was used in the French intensive gardening technique, made popular in Paris market gardens in the late 1800s. *Cloche,* in fact, is the French word for "bell," and the first cloches were simple, glass, bell-shaped domes that covered individual plants. Today, bells are made of glass or plastic. Glass might be prohibitively expensive, but you can make your own plastic ones using large, transparent juice or milk containers with the bottoms cut off and the lids unscrewed when ventilation is desired.

When using any type of cloche or cold frame, I am much more diligent about watering, because all of them prevent rain from reaching the plants, drying out the soil surprisingly quickly.

GARDEN STRUCTURES

Season-extending tools like cloches and cold frames can enhance our sometimes scarce maritime sunlight, but I also use other structural techniques to capture more rays, dry the soil, and get good air circulation. Creating a permanent base or frame for the cloche or cold frame can make it easier to use those devices. Two additional techniques are raised beds, which can enhance soil conditions, and trellises, which can help ripen fruit and reduce the likelihood of disease.

The most common structure in a vegetable garden may be the raised bed, often made of wood or stone. The traditional raised bed is simply a mound of earth; often it is initially "double-dug" to work compost and manure more deeply into the earth and to create a more porous soil. (For the best primer on the valuable double-digging technique, seek out a copy of *How to Grow More Vegetables* by John Jeavons.) But a raised bed that is bordered by stones, wood, or plastic lumber can be a great help to the maritime gardener in other ways. The soil will dry out more quickly in the spring, for instance. Heat radiating from the stones can increase nighttime soil temperatures, too, which is important for seed germination.

Although there are many techniques for building raised beds, here are a few tips:

❧ Make sure you can reach to the center of your raised bed from each side. Stepping into the bed will compact the soil, and you want to avoid compaction to improve its tilth (which is the quality of the soil).

❧ Consider the materials from the standpoint of environmental sustainability. Don't use lumber treated with chemicals; they can leach into the soil, be taken up by your food crops, and end up in your body as well.

❧ If you have scrap lumber, stones, bricks, or pavers sitting around, try to reuse those as raised-bed walls. Low cost and recycling are mantras of sustainable gardening.

❧ If you're bringing in materials, consider which ones will best handle wet maritime conditions: concrete blocks and engineered lumber made of recycled plastic are two great choices. Concrete is virtually indestructible, but lumber set on its edge takes up much less space. Untreated lumber in contact with the soil will last perhaps five years before rot will take over.

One benefit of building raised beds out of wood or plastic lumber is that you can attach flat copper strips to the sides or top of the frame, which will act as an effective slug and snail barrier. Frames of wood or plastic lumber are also useful to hold cloche attachments or, if built to exacting specifications, to serve as the base for a cold frame. If you're considering a raised bed that will integrate one of these season extenders, remember to orient it properly for maximum solar gain.

Finally, consider supplying your garden with a variety of trellises. Trellises are a key component of the maritime gardener's approach to garden diseases. In a cool, moist climate, they help provide good air circulation around plants, which is especially important at ground level. They also allow you to keep the foliage from becoming too dense, which will prevent or minimize fungal diseases such as blight and powdery mildew that can stunt plants or cause fruit to rot.

You might need a 7-foot trellis for Tall Telephone peas, and a sturdy one to hold the prolific vines of the Chadwick's cherry tomato. Smaller squashes like Red Kuri could be grown on a tent-shaped trellis, their rust-colored globes safely cradled by nylon stockings recycled for that use. Hog fencing, which has 2- to 3-inch openings and is larger and sturdier than chicken wire, can be cut to desired lengths and stapled to posts, and then stored after the season by simply pulling the staples and rolling it up.

A stack of recycled bamboo stakes—preferably 10 to 12 feet or longer—will serve for many seasons to handle your Cherokee Trail of Tears pole beans. Lay five poles together and bind them with twine a foot from one end, then turn the assemblage upright and form it into a teepee shape. Secure each pole to stakes in the ground, and plant beans at the base of the poles.

Maximizing the sun, aiding air circulation, and helping the soil become workable earlier while retaining moisture and nutrients are all unique challenges for the maritime gardener. Whether you're using age-old techniques or the latest garden-store products, your heirloom vegetables will be more likely to thrive if you give some attention to site selection, season extenders, and useful structures.

PILGRIMS PROGRESSED WITH HOT BEDS

Want to create a winter garden like your agrarian ancestors? Make a "hot bed" with manure and a cold-frame structure.

Wesley Green, garden historian for the Colonial Williamsburg Foundation, told me that "in 1577, the first English gardening book discusses the hot bed, which uses manure to compost under the ground and send heat up." The technique was brought to the New World by early European colonists and can, in fact, be seen today by winter visitors to Colonial Williamsburg on the coast of Virginia.

Green described how each year he and his assistants stake out the dimensions of their cold frame, dig a trench 30 inches deep, fill it two-thirds full with fresh horse manure, packed quite tightly, and cover that with a foot of tightly packed soil. The manure will slowly decompose, sending heat to the surface as it does. The cold frame, with wooden sides and a glass top, covers the hot bed. With this method, Green can start plants in January in a region where winter means frozen ground and regular snowfall.

In our maritime climate, we could use a hot bed to store tropical potted plants, to sprout seedlings in pots, or even to start seeds in the ground, although it's important to make sure that the manure will have decomposed before the plant roots reach it.

Friends and neighbors bond over gardening when building a community garden or sharing seeds. And when you practice seed-saving and year-round gardening, your garden helps you move closer to self-sufficiency. Here are some seasonal ideas to focus your gardening energies.

If you want to increase the peas, love, and understanding in your neighborhood, start a community garden. You will cultivate much more than tomatoes on that abandoned lot or unused park space.

Here are the seeds of a world more in harmony: an inner-city child learns that the simple act of a bee visiting a flower can result in wonderful food for our table; a new immigrant who is barely getting by becomes an inspirational community leader; a group of people working together one summer delivers more than 2,000 pounds of nutritious, fresh produce to a food bank. These are all acts I've witnessed by being part of a community garden. Over many years of involvement, I've also made a number of friends, participated in many celebrations, and supplied my family's table with an incredible volume of produce.

SPRING: SPROUT A COMMUNITY GARDEN

Get started by searching for existing resources in your community. Many major cities and even good-sized towns have programs, often run by their parks departments, that provide land and the basic operating needs. Vancouver (BC), Seattle, Portland, and San Francisco all have vibrant, growing efforts (see Resources). Great advice can come from existing programs.

Here are some basic things to consider:

LAND You'll need it contributed, loaned, leased, or purchased. Look for municipal land, unused church or school grounds, or abandoned city lots. The property should get at least six hours of full sun a day for good growing conditions. You could even garden in raised beds on the roof of a new green-built office complex. Most often the land is leased, with a five-year contract providing some assurance that your initial hard work will not be wasted. You can also start a nonprofit to raise money to buy or lease land.

INTERESTED PARTIES Consider who else could benefit from the garden, and discover their wants and needs. The criteria and design will be different depending on whether you're greening a public eyesore, providing a patch of dirt for apartment dwellers, or helping nursing home residents gain horticultural therapy.

MATERIALS You'll need tools, seed, watering hoses, possibly materials to build raised beds, and perhaps even structures such as tool sheds and compost bins. You'll probably want to do soil tests; most likely you'll have to improve the soil, which on some sites can be a major undertaking. You'll also need a water source and pathways. A central gathering place is a highly recommended amenity, for which you'll want pavers, trellises, and seating. Consider how you'll pay for all this; many gardens use a combination of garden plot fees, grant money, and municipal underwriting. Some hold fundraising events.

Any new garden will benefit from planning. If possible, draft a design in advance of planting. Creating the "hardscape" of entries, paths, composting areas, a storage area for bulk materials, and amenities will be much easier if done before gardening begins, especially if the site needs grading or if a watering system is to be installed.

As you can see, there are so many considerations in starting a community garden that this list is just a hen-scratch in the dirt. The American Community Gardening Association's website, www.communitygarden.org, is a great help. Although the spade-work may be daunting, this can be one of the most rewarding and fruitful efforts for yourself and your community.

Have you considered saving your own seed for next year's garden? Or do you wonder why you should bother, because it's so much easier to buy from your favorite seed catalog, and aren't you keeping them in business by buying their seed?

   Today, even the question of saving seed is complex, for farmers as well as backyard gardeners. Farmers since ancient times have practiced seed saving, but these days seed can be patented. One industrial agriculture conglomerate, Monsanto, is now suing farmers who've saved their own seed if some of Monsanto's seed has somehow made its way into their fields, or even if genes from the patented seed have entered the farmer's saved seed through cross-pollination.

   Such an incredible situation has not happened with home gardeners who save seed—at least not yet. And though the best reason to buy commercial seed is to keep the few remaining gardener-focused seed companies in business, there are good reasons to save your own seed:

DESIGN

SUMMER: CLOSE THE LOOP BY SAVING SEED

❧ You can assure yourself that your favorite variety will not disappear. A great percentage of heirloom varieties have been lost, and the trend continues. Keeping a variety alive—especially if it's scarce—is the best effort you can make to ensure continual plant diversity. Your contribution is enhanced if you share seed through a seed-saving organization.

❧ Your seed will be more attuned to your ecological conditions. Proper seed saving can result in a more vigorous strain of plants because you will be selecting the specimens that have grown best in your soil and your climate.

❧ You'll save money on seed purchases.

❧ You'll reduce your "carbon footprint"—the ecological impact that comes from having seeds harvested, processed, packaged, and shipped to you.

To take your seed saving to the community level, join a seed-savers' network, such as the Iowa-based nonprofit Seed Savers Exchange. You can trade seeds with other members, contribute to the network's seed bank, and financially support its efforts to ensure biodiversity. To further support advocacy and commercial seed diversity efforts, become a member of the Organic Seed Alliance, based in Port Townsend, Washington.

Learn to save seed: The basics of seed-saving are included for many of the individual plant listings in this book, but for a complete education on the subject, see the definitive book *Seed to Seed* by Suzanne Ashworth (see Resources).

SEED-SAVING HISTORY: FROM A RUSSIAN
TRAGEDY TO AN ARCTIC DEEP FREEZE

It's been called a "Noah's Ark" and a "doomsday vault," but the optimist in me hopes that the Svalbard Global Seed Vault will never have to live up to those names.

The massive seed bank, drilled into the permafrost 400 feet below the surface of a Norwegian island, opened in 2008 and is intended to hold 4.5 million seed samples, contributed from around the world. At temperatures near zero degrees Fahrenheit, the seeds should remain viable for many years, and will be replaced periodically by the seed banks that deposited them there. This project is the latest effort to place the world's plant diversity in safekeeping, a practice that is happening at approximately 1,400 seed banks around the world. The United States operates its own bank, called the National Center for Genetic Resources Preservation, in Fort Collins, Colorado. Nonprofit seed banks, like Seed Savers Exchange, augment government efforts.

The father of modern seed saving was botanist Nikolai Vavilov, whose research institute in St. Petersburg, Russia, contains 320,000 seed samples. He traveled the world on preservation missions in the 1920s and 1930s. He developed the widely accepted theory that cultivated plants have a "center of origin," and mapped eight areas where he believed most of the world's crops had been domesticated. He was persecuted by the Soviet state and died of starvation in prison in 1943.

World War II saw a tragic but heroic episode at his Institute. During the 28-month siege of Leningrad by Axis powers, starvation was rampant in the city (now known as St. Petersburg). Although surrounded by edible seed, many of the Institute's scientists died of starvation as they continued their work, rather than consume the valuable seed collection.

**AUTUMN:
NEXT HOLIDAY,
DINE FROM
YOUR GARDEN**

It is a noble undertaking for maritime gardeners to put our own vegetables on the table for holiday meals, and it is not that difficult to achieve. We've already discussed, in Chapter 3, how site selection, drainage, and season-extending tools such as cloches and cold frames can help. You also must have proper soil structure and nutrition, because plants will suffer more winter stress in poor soil. But the trickiest part of all might be sowing seeds at the right time so that the plants will mature in winter.

Some winter-harvest vegetables have long seasons that call for sowing in the late spring and are nearly mature when the cold weather hits. Others are short-season crops that are sown in early fall so that the plants will have well-set roots and enough top growth to weather the winter. Some will overwinter and mature in early spring. All plantings and growth rates are subject to your own climate and conditions, so experimentation is necessary to see what will work best for you.

In general, sowing for winter harvest takes place from May through September, although in warmer regions of the maritime Northwest, fall sowing can extend through October. You might plant carrots and beets in June for a cornucopia of root veggies at Thanksgiving, aim for a New Year's stir-fry with August-planted spinach, or plant lettuce in September and offer your sweetheart an ultra-local salad on Valentine's Day.

Choosing the proper variety of each winter vegetable is key to success. Some varieties grow more slowly and are hardier than others. Many catalogs will indicate whether the variety is good for fall or winter growing.

If year-round gardening is currently too much for you, you can still eat food from your garden all year. Grow some vegetables that store well—winter squash, potatoes, onions, and garlic—and then pull them out for a holiday meal. Or, if you're ready to learn a new skill, there's always the option of preserving your garden's bounty through freezing, drying, and canning.

Two great resources for more information are *Winter Gardening in the Maritime Northwest* by Binda Colebrook and *The Maritime Northwest Garden Guide,* published by Seattle Tilth Association (see Bibliography).

WINTER: HOST A SEED EXCHANGE

Every winter I get together with a group of friends to discuss the upcoming gardening season and collectively order seeds. It's an opportunity to discuss what grew well in last year's garden, share ideas about techniques, and commiserate about the weather. It's also a great way to deepen our connection to the plants and heighten our awareness of varieties we haven't tried. More important, though, it's a way for us to share the bounty that comes from palm-sized packets of seeds, and to count out the little nuggets of life that will bring us food and flavors and flowers in the coming months.

A few simple steps will get this tradition started. First, of course, you need a group of people who grow their own food. This is easy to find if you have a plot in a community garden, or if you are a member of a local nonprofit organization that focuses on food gardening.

Schedule a potluck meeting at someone's home on a winter evening after the seed catalogs have arrived. Ask all the participants to bring their catalogs and their own seed collections—both commercial seed left over from previous years and seed saved from their own plants. If it's the latter, try to have them be sure of the variety. It's also important to know the age of the seed; in no case should home-stored seed that is more than five years old be relied upon for planting. Life is too short to plant old seed.

SOME COMMONLY GROWN
WINTER VEGETABLES

*Heirloom varieties particularly noted for winter growing
are named in parentheses.*

Arugula
Asian Greens (Mizuna, Tatsoi, Green-in-the-Snow)
Beets (Lutz)
Broccoli (Purple Sprouting)
Cabbage (January King)
Carrots
Chard (Fordhook)
Corn Salad
Kale (Russian Red)
Leeks
Lettuce
Spinach (Giant Winter)

When everyone has assembled and gotten reacquainted over
dinner, begin the meeting by assigning one person to each major
seed catalog from which you'll purchase. The person in charge
of each catalog order will tally up the requests for seed from that
catalog.

Since most catalogs are arranged alphabetically, simply begin
paging through the vegetables, discussing any that people want to
order. Comments will fly about a favorite bean, or which supplier
has the best chard. Along the way, each person can delve into his
or her own seed collection to share any seed already in hand rather
than purchase it. You'll need a supply of small paper envelopes for
sharing (plastic bags should be avoided).

After the lists are made, orders are placed to each seed company, and the group reconvenes in a few weeks, once the seed shipments have been received. In this way, people always get fresh seed, never more than they can use in a season or two, and the cost and shipping are kept to a minimum.

When you hold the seed exchange over multiple years, you get to know which varieties are consistent winners, and the sharing of techniques and successes makes everyone a better gardener. But the real power comes from the process of counting out seeds and packaging them up for sharing. Through this simple act, a bond is being created among people and between gardens that supports everyone involved and includes them in the age-old practice of gardening in a community.

HEIRLOOM
VEGETABLE
LIST

Each of the plant descriptions below offers basic information on cultivation, harvest, storage, and seed saving, followed by a list of heirloom varieties of that vegetable, chosen for their compatibility with a maritime climate as well as for their consistent availability through one or more seed sources. Even so, you may not always find these varieties available. If not, I encourage you to experiment with other heirlooms.

My advice on growing is necessarily quite general, and should be just the beginning of your gardening exploration. Many more comprehensive books exist that detail successful cultivation methods, from germination to seed saving. Seed catalogs also provide great tips, and they list details that are not included here, such as days to maturity, seed spacing, and combating pests or diseases. Please see the Bibliography for guidance to other garden books and the Resources section for a list of seed sources.

ARUGULA

Eruca vesicaria sativa and *Diplotaxis muralis*

You might think arugula was a recent addition to the salad bar, having sprung up in the last two decades in gourmet salad mixes popularized by small farms serving restaurants and farmers markets. However, it made the list in a classic American garden text, Fearing Burr Jr.'s comprehensive 1863 book *The Field and Garden Vegetables of America* (see Bibliography), so gardeners and cooks with a taste for some zing in their salads have been munching arugula at least since the Civil War.

Originating in southern Europe, it is also known as roquette, rocket, and garden rocket, and it has been shooting up out of the ground in my garden for years as though fired from underneath. In fact, one seed packet is all that many gardeners will ever need to buy if they practice a bit of seed saving or just tolerate some wildness in their beds.

There are two genera of arugula, although they both belong to the mustard family. *Eruca vesicaria sativa* is the cultivated garden arugula, and *Diplotaxis muralis* is the wild arugula.

Arugula seeds can be sown heavily and thinned to 4 inches apart. It is best picked and eaten at a tender young stage, when the leaves approach 2 inches. Its arrow-shaped, pale spears become darker green and more deeply lobed with age. An upright, branching, dark-purple stem delivers creamy pale-yellow or white four-lobed flowers streaked with brown veins. The edible buds and flowers dress up a salad and provide a nutty, often hotter version of the peppery arugula flavor. Primarily a salad green, arugula is also great chopped into stir-fries, soups, or stews, and larger leaves can be braised. It is aromatic and herbaceous with eggs, and wonderful in a frittata.

Rocket

Like most leafy greens, arugula does best in a nutrient-rich, loamy soil. Plant in spring or fall, and water regularly, especially at its young stage. Summer plantings are quick to bolt. Grow in partial to full sun. It is a cool-season, hardy annual, and will tolerate mild winters if well established, so in our maritime climate it can be planted and grown year-round. It's naturally vigorous, but may be side-dressed with nitrogen fertilizer in less-than-optimal conditions. On older plants, or ones weathering a drought or a tough winter, the leaves will become tough and strong-flavored.

CULTIVATION

Younger leaves are much more tender, so cut them as soon as they've sized up to 2 inches or so. Pick individual leaves, choose small plants as you thin the rows, or scissor back the top growth in the cut-and-come-again method. Brief refrigerator storage of two to three days is possible, but arugula is spiciest and crispest when harvested fresh each time you make a salad.

HARVEST AND STORAGE

If you leave a bit of it to flower, arugula will deposit seeds around the garden from cylindrical pods on rangy stems. One plant can become a bushy 2 feet high and a foot wide, with numerous seed pods. Left to open and drop, the seeds will readily germinate. To save seed, cut stems when the pods are half-brittle, place them in a paper bag to fully dry, and then crush the pods and allow the small, black, round seeds to roll away from the chaff.

SEED SAVING

One plant that's gone to seed can provide an entire bed of arugula. Allow the seed to partially dry on the plant, but before the seed pods open, uproot it and lay the entire plant to dry over a prepared bed. A dense forest of seedlings will soon provide an ample arugula bed that can be thinned or sheared for salads.

TIP

VARIETIES

Rocket The common garden arugula, *Eruca vesicaria sativa,* is characterized by longer, arrow-shaped leaves on a larger plant than the wild arugula. Its vigorous upright habit, with flower stalks that can reach 24 inches, makes this an eye-catching plant in the salad greens bed.

Sylvetta A variety of *Diplotaxis muralis,* this wild arugula has dark green, heavily lobed leaves that grow to 8 inches in a rosette close to the soil. The plant develops more slowly than its domesticated cousin, but it is also slower to bolt, so it will deliver a spicy-hot salad element for a long season.

ASIAN GREENS

Brassica rapa and
B. juncea

Cool climates are especially suitable for growing hardy, nutrient-dense, leafy greens. Gardeners who enjoy variety will want to include some Asian brassicas—such as mustard greens, Chinese cabbage, or sprout-producing broccoli—along with their other leafy vegetables. Asian immigrants likely brought many of these to the U.S., although there is some history of missionaries carrying brassica seeds home when returning from Asia. It is difficult to find the origin stories of these vegetables, although many have been named for the town (such as Osaka Purple) or area where they were first cultivated. The colors, shapes, and variations from European salad greens, kales, cabbages, and broccoli provide delightful discovery.

Tatsoi

These choices also will offer variety to winter or early-spring dinners made from the garden. Sturdy Chinese pak choi, with its loose leaves and taste similar to that of its cousin bok choi (which grows as a head), will add crunch and succulence to a stir-fry. Tender mizuna infuses delicate spiciness into a fresh green salad. The spoon-shaped leaves of tatsoi add a mustardy zing to a hearty soup.

Asian salad greens like a well-cultivated seedbed with good moisture retention for their shallow roots. A balanced fertilizer or a layer of compost dug into the soil will give them a good start. Most of the tender greens are best grown from seed, while the sturdier brassicas are more tolerant of transplanting. If you're starting

CULTIVATION

indoors or purchasing salad greens as starts, plant in small clumps rather than trying to separate individual seedlings.

When planting, keep in mind ultimate size and spacing needs. Many greens grow great as row crops, but some can require a foot or more between plants to achieve full size. They do best when planted in cooler weather (some seeds will germinate only at lower temperatures), so plant in early spring for summer use, and in late summer for fall and winter crops. Plants that are sizing up at the peak of summer are likely to bolt quickly. Because growing conditions are harsher in winter, keep plants well weeded and protected to aid development. Some will go to seed after an abrupt temperature drop. On the positive side, the flavor of many greens is brought out by cool nights or a light frost. In areas with a hard winter, protect greens in a cloche or get an early spring start by planting them under a cold frame.

HARVEST AND STORAGE

Snip individual shoots or leaves, or shear a row, leaving at least two sets of leaves above the cotyledon leaves (the first set of leaves that appear when the plant sprouts) to support regrowth. Because the various plants in this category have different growth habits, harvest methods are offered in more detail for each variety. Storage of greens is problematic; they are best if eaten within hours of harvest. If necessary, refrigerate them unwashed in a loose plastic bag, and only for a day or two. Sturdier cuttings such as pak choi bunches and brassica shoots will last a bit longer than tender individual leaves.

SEED SAVING

Most Chinese cabbages and mustards are biennial, meaning that they will normally go to seed in their second season (although they can flower and set seed at the end of one long season). To overwinter, move some hardy specimens to a protected edge of the garden; or pot them up and store in a cool place, water occasionally, and then plant them out into the garden the second spring. The plants will flower and produce seed pods, which will turn light brown when dry. Caution: Different varieties of *B. rapa* will cross with each other, as will members of *B. juncea.* Since isolation distances are not practical in most home gardens, save only one variety of each for seed each year.

A winter salad from the garden can range far beyond lettuce—in fact, try skipping lettuce altogether. Create a complex mix of flavors with young Asian greens combined with leaves of European greens such as arugula, chard, corn salad, and radicchio. East meets West!

VARIETIES OF ASIAN CABBAGE, KALE, AND GREENS (B. RAPA)

Kalian

This tender Chinese kale produces edible leaves and flower buds on upright stalks. It is crisp, tender, and mild. It has attractive white flowers and pale green leaves and can be cooked like broccoli. As with other kales, start it a bit earlier for fall harvest.

Mizuna

Feathery, serrated soft-green leaves spring up in a tight bunch with white stems to form this vigorous yet delicate Japanese green. Mild but with a slight mustardy flavor, it is popular in salads but also can be cooked like spinach. The plant can size up to 12 inches or more, and can keep producing well into the winter, regrowing readily after cuttings. It is vigorous under nearly all conditions except heat.

Pak Choi

Also known as Chinese cabbage, this sturdy green has an upright growth habit, with shapely white or pale green stalks, cupped and layered, ending in loose, spoon-shaped leaves of deep green. It has received mention in American garden books at least since the

1860s, possibly arriving with returning missionaries from China, where it has been cultivated since the fifth century. Its cousin bok choi (or bok choy) has a more heading habit.

VARIETIES OF MUSTARD GREENS *(B. JUNCEA)*

Green-in-the-Snow
Leaves have jagged edges and are dark green, with some almost black. Very fast-growing, vigorous, and hardiest of all the mustards. Young leaves are pleasantly spicy; older ones may be too hot for the palate.

Miike
This Chinese mustard grows to 15 inches, with crinkled, purple-veined leaves. Older leaves may be strong-flavored, so it's best to use younger, smaller ones.

Osaka Purple
A striking purple blush along the top half of the leaves distinguishes this mildly spicy variety. Stems are succulent and light green. Individual leaves can be larger (up to 6 by 8 inches), crinkled, and fan-shaped; outer leaves can turn maroon in cold weather. It is slow to bolt after overwintering.

Tatsoi
One of the most handsome winter greens, tatsoi is a spinachlike mustard that grows in a spreading rosette to form layers of dark green leaves, which combat cold weather by hugging the soil. Its name translates as "February vegetable." Leaves are glossy and deeply ribbed, with a pleasing roundness. Texture is tough, but taste is mild and succulent, becoming better after a frost. Also known as tah tsai.

BEANS

Phaseolus vulgaris,
P. coccineus, and
Vicia faba

Beans are simply amazing. On the American table, their uses are diverse and accommodating. We eat them in all stages of their development: slender green pods with immature seeds, fully formed bean seeds shelled while green, and dried seeds that are reconstituted in cooking. In the garden, their growth habits will suit many situations; and they can produce heavy yields. Their third attribute is beauty: striking flowers, vigorous bushes or vines, a rainbow of colorful pods and, of course, a mosaic of colors and patterns in the dried bean seeds.

The sheer number of varieties means that listings in most seed catalogs or books (including this one) will be a drop in the bucket. In 2009, there were more than 800 varieties of beans sold in commercial seed catalogs, Seed Savers Exchange members were trading more than 1500 varieties, and perhaps hundreds more are being preserved at SSE. John Withee of Maine, credited as the father of the heirloom bean movement, had over 1000 varieties in his collection, which was turned over to SSE in 1981, shortly before his death.

Beans have a history nearly as long as civilization. They've been found dating to 8000 BC in archaeological digs in Peru. Beans have been used as valuable trading currency and as colorful jewelry; the ancient Greeks even used fava beans as voting tokens. Many beans originated in South and Central America, were taken to Europe by explorers, and then were brought to the United States. A number of varieties, such as Cherokee Trail of Tears, originated in North America and were cultivated by native people prior to the arrival of settlers. Native Americans planted them with corn and squash, creating synergy among the "Three Sisters" who help one another: corn provides a bean trellis, large squash leaves shade the soil and keep down the weeds, and the vining beans bind all the sisters together while keeping the soil fertile by fixing nitrogen onto the roots.

Today, well-loved heirloom beans exist in almost every region and have become staples in gardens across the country. Many gardeners have a few favorite varieties that they grow every year. But a deeper look into the world of beans should be inspiration enough to try yet another of these excellent legumes.

CULTIVATION Many edibles are described as easy to grow, but that is especially true of beans. You will be off to a good start simply by paying attention to space needs (how large will the bush get? how tall should the trellis be?) and planting dates (beans don't germinate well if the soil temperature is below 60°F). This is a vegetable that children enjoy planting, even if the final product is not among their favorite foods. Beans have large, attractive seeds, they pop out of the ground fast, and their lore—think "Jack and the Beanstalk"—is well established in children's literature. Children who help grow beans could easily change their mind about eating them.

Beans are always planted from seed, not starts. Bush beans should be planted 2 to 4 inches apart in rows 18 to 24 inches apart. Pole beans should be planted three to a pole. The seedbed should be well cultivated, with compost added for moisture retention. Beans are fairly light feeders and will do fine with a balanced fertilizer mixed in at planting. Additional fertilizer is not always necessary, and in fact can be detrimental; too much nitrogen will produce leggy, leafy bush beans with few flowers. Regular water during early development is essential because beans have shallow roots. Overhead watering is discouraged—it will expose the plants to diseases such as rust, mildew, and blight. When plants are three inches high, mulch with an organic compost. Plant in succession every two to three weeks to lengthen the harvest.

Dragon's Tongue

To ensure the highest productivity from your fresh green beans, harvest regularly—almost daily for some varieties. Capture the *haricots verts,* or French filet beans, when they are still very slender. Other "snap" bush beans (those whose pods are eaten whole, with just the ends snapped off) can be allowed to fill their pods with more mature seeds, as can the snap pole beans, but only to the point where their pods turn from fleshy to stringy or fibrous. Shelling beans ("shellies"), also known as horticultural beans, can be eaten as snap beans when very young, but most varieties are best when the plump pods are shelled and the beans eaten green.

HARVEST AND STORAGE

Regular picking and eating of bush and pole beans will help you refine the process to achieve the height of ripeness. A bonus: Regular picking encourages more flowers to form on the plants, thus increasing productivity.

To harvest fresh shelling beans, pick individual pods as they ripen. Fava beans *(Vicia faba)* will tell you when they're ready to pick, as the pods change from pointing up to drooping downward. Runner beans *(Phaseolus coccineus)* are ready to pick when the seeds are visibly swelling in their long pods. Pods of either type can be left on the plant if you want dry shelling beans.

Dry shelling beans are more forgiving of harvest timing. For bush beans, harvest takes place when 90 percent of the leaves have fallen off the plant and you see a shell or two start to open. Bush beans dry uniformly, but with pole beans, expect the bottom pods to dry first. Depending on weather conditions, dry shelling beans may need to be harvested before the plants have died back and the shells are completely dry. If necessary, continue drying under cover.

To dry an entire bush-bean plant, pull it out by the roots and then lay it flat or hang it. When pods are entirely dry and pop open readily, thresh the beans by beating the bush from side to side in a bucket. You can also put the whole plant into a burlap bag and then walk on it or paddle it to separate the beans. Spread out bean seeds on a dry surface in a cool, shady place. When thoroughly dry, a bean seed won't dent when you bite down on it.

SEED SAVING   Beans are the ideal plant for beginner seed-savers. They're easy to save and use and, when properly dried, they have great shelf life. They self-pollinate, so the seeds should produce the true variety. However, to minimize the potential of cross-pollination from bees, separate bean varieties by 25 feet, or grow a different tall plant between varieties. This is especially important for runner beans. To prevent fungus growth, store thoroughly dry beans in breathable containers, such as envelopes or paper bags, always labeled properly with the variety and date.

Grow better beans (and peas, too) and improve your soil nutrients by using a legume inoculant when planting. The inoculant consists of a rhizobium, a soil bacterium that helps the roots of the legume "fix" nitrogen, the process in which the plant pulls nitrogen from the air and attaches it in nodules onto its roots. The plant uses this nitrogen for growth, and releases the remaining amount into the soil. Moisten the seeds and coat with the powdery inoculant right before planting, or sprinkle granular inoculant in the furrow when planting.

TIP

VARIETIES

The venerable nineteenth-century French book *The Vegetable Garden* by Messrs. Vilmorin-Andrieux described Black Coco as tall-growing and productive, but rather late, and added, "As a variety, it does not possess much interest." On that last point, I beg to differ, as this has been one of the most delectable and reliable dry bush beans in my garden. Unlike the Blue Coco, another French heirloom that has purple pods, Black Coco has seeds darker than its cocoa-inspired name, wrapped in a tender, round green pod. Plants are compact, to 24 inches tall.

Black Coco

The favorite fava for cool regions (it comes from England), Broad Windsor produces 6-inch pods with four to six beans each on sturdy, upright plants that grow to 36 inches. The plant thrives even in a wet climate, and is often grown as an overwintering bean as well as for spring planting. The broad bean is a succulent side dish on the winter menu—shelled, sautéed, or boiled, and served

Broad Windsor

with just a bit of butter and salt. Very popular in early America, it was grown by Thomas Jefferson.

Cannellino This is the premier Tuscan white kidney bean that is dried and delectable in minestrone. When cooked long and slowly, it can melt into a flavorful, creamy consistency. Plants are bush habit, up to 3 feet, and pods can be 6 to 7 inches long.

Cherokee Trail of Tears This dry pole bean bears the most tragic story of any heirloom. It was a staple of the Cherokee Indian nation, and was carried with them when the tribe was driven by the U.S. Army from the southeast states to Oklahoma. The forced march through the Smoky Mountains in the winter of 1838 reportedly left 4,000 graves by the trail. Green 6-inch pods with purple streaks yield flavorful fresh beans or jet-black dry beans.

Dragon's Tongue A beautiful wax bush bean that is very versatile, doing double duty as a fresh snap bean or as a shellie. The flattish pods begin pale green and then develop purple streaks and stains against a dusky yellow background. Compact plants grow to 15 inches. Also known as Dragon Langerie, it came to the U.S. from the Netherlands. Dried beans are light brown with dark brown spots.

Fin de Bagnols A delectable French filet-style *(haricot vert)* bean, this snap bean ripens early on 2-foot bushes that are productive in cooler climates. Also called "shoestring bean," it's been a favorite in American gardens since the 1800s. Harvest the slender, round pods just when they reach 5 to 6 inches.

Italian Romano This familiar snap pole variety is the broad, flat green bean seen on so many Italian tables. Its smooth pods are stringless and meaty, but with a delicate texture. Cook it lightly for best flavor and consistency. Freezes well.

New England gave us this distinctive bush bean, commonly harvested dry and used in baked-bean dishes. On a compact, 2-foot plant grow 4- to 5-inch pods of medium-sized, speckled beans. Seeds are white with maroon blotching on the inner curve and speckles overall. It is also known as Trout, possibly because it was developed and introduced by Virginia farmer Jacob Trout.

Jacob's Cattle

Also known as Old Homestead, this snap pole bean is earlier and tastier than many other varieties, and is rust resistant. It has white flowers on airy, open 7-foot vines that produce 7- to 10-inch green pods. It was called Texas Pole when mentioned in an 1864 edition of *The Country Gentleman* magazine, according to the Baker Creek Heirloom Seeds catalog, and became Kentucky Wonder when introduced by the James J. H. Gregory & Sons seed house in 1877. It can also be used as a dry bean.

Kentucky Wonder

This beautiful runner bean has been in American gardens since the early 1800s, but it has grown in England since 1596, and was reportedly named for the made-up appearance of Queen Elizabeth I. It delivers showy pink and red flowers with white centers on vigorous vines that will twine up a trellis counterclockwise. It can reach 6 feet in height, producing flat pods up to 10 inches long. The rough-skinned yet tender beans can be eaten fresh, or left to mature and dry into three-quarter-inch-long hearty beans that have maroon sprays over a buff background.

Painted Lady

The standard runner bean in many gardens, this variety produces an energetic vine that fills the sky to 8 feet or more. Its abundant, red-orange flowers produce fuzzy pods that some people consider the most flavorful among all the varieties. They can be eaten green as snap beans. The dried beans, used by Native Americans in jewelry, are mottled dark red to purple; they add meatiness, flavor, and color to soups and stews.

Scarlet Runner

Wren's Egg A fresh shelling pole bean that has buff-colored seed with streaks of red reminiscent of the bird's egg. It is one of the largest of its type, producing a broad, oval seed, but the pods can be eaten fresh as snap beans at 5 inches. Possibly originating in Chile and also known as London Horticultural, it dates in the U.S. to 1825.

BEETS

Beta vulgaris

The deep red root of a beet is, to me, one of the most intriguing of all vegetables. Like other root crops, it develops partially unseen, its size and heft revealed only when it's plucked from the soil. It provides a curious, satisfying bounty, wrapped in a package that bleeds when it's cut but can be kept and stored for a long time without concern. It freely gives up leaves for us while developing its root, calmly sending up another batch of leaves to fuel its growth.

I grew up eating pickled beets, but the beets from my garden mostly go into the oven to be roasted, skinned, and chopped as a side dish or the basis for a salad. Beets also can be boiled. The younger ones can be eaten raw, thinly sliced or grated into salads.

Beets originated in Europe's Mediterranean regions, where references to their cultivation for greens go back as early as the thirteenth century. The roots were originally used as cattle fodder. Sometime later they began to be eaten, but in Colonial America the beet was outshone by the turnip. In fact, plant historian William Woys Weaver notes that beets were known as "blood turnips" up until the 1800s. They're also known as "beetroot," and their relatives include the sugar beet, grown to produce refined sugar, and the mangel-wurzel, a stock-feed variety.

Detroit Dark Red

Like carrots and radishes, beet varieties can produce roots of different shapes and colors. Most early varieties had pointed roots like turnips, with the round and flat-bottomed ones being developed more recently. The flesh can range from yellow to crimson to burgundy, or even, in the case of Chioggia (pronounced "kee-OH-gee-a"), concentric rings of pink and white. Today some varieties are prized primarily for their greens, which bear significant resemblance to their close relative chard. Typically, beet greens have deep red stems with red ribs and veins and a gently ruffled leaf edge, but the leaves can range from light green to ruby to dark red. Whatever the color, top or bottom, beets make a handsome as well as tasty garden addition.

Grow only from seed, sow directly into the garden, and resist transplanting. Beets require a loamy, well-draining soil, and will not do well in clay or compacted earth. Dig in a balanced fertilizer below the row at planting time. Plant 1 inch apart, in rows a foot apart. Beets need regular water; rings in the root (called "zoning") can develop from lack of water or extreme temperature changes. Plant twice a year, in spring and fall.

CULTIVATION

Weed regularly, and gently cultivate the soil between rows to encourage root development. Thin to each variety's specified spacing, but at least 3 to 4 inches apart, to achieve full size.

HARVEST AND STORAGE

Cut beet greens regularly; baby greens are great for salads, while full-sized leaves can be chopped and steamed or sautéed. Harvest roots when beets have achieved the average size for their variety; medium-sized beets are often sweeter and more flavorful than larger ones. Beets can be overwintered in the ground under a thick layer of mulch, but this technique does not work as well in areas with heavy winter rains, and beets stored in the ground can be chewed by voles. Beets also can be stored in sand or sawdust in a cool, dark area, and will keep in the refrigerator for weeks.

SEED SAVING

The beet, like the carrot, is biennial, so it will make seed only in its second year. Some seed-savers advise choosing promising specimens to grow for seed (best to have a number of plants to maintain genetic viability) and then transplanting them out of the way, to the edge of the vegetable bed or a perennial bed. Because the seed stalk may grow to 4 feet, it may need staking. The seeds form along the stalk, in rough, irregular clusters. As the lower seeds on the stalk turn brown and start to dry, harvest the plants and place in paper bags; when they are dry, thresh the seeds through a screen. Beets will cross-pollinate with other beets and with chard, so each must be isolated to get seed true to its variety.

TIP

Do not peel or pierce beets before cooking. Simply trim the tops to within an inch of the root, and trim the tail of the root to that length as well. Cooking whole retains the nutrients and sweetness. Roast in the oven and, when tender, plunge into cold water for a few seconds, after which the skins should slip off.

VARIETIES

Chioggia

Possibly the most beautiful beet in presentation, this variety, also known as Bassano, comes from the Italian coastal town of Chioggia on the Adriatic Sea south of Venice. Green tops and red stems spring from a 3-inch, wine-red globe. When the beet is sliced, concentric rings of pink and white are revealed. The colors fade in cooking, but harvested small and sliced thin, this beet can be a delightful salad addition; I've seen it called the "candy cane beet" in a restaurant holiday salad.

Detroit Dark Red

For many years the standard variety for home gardeners, this is a flavorful and reliable producer of both greens and roots. Dark-green leaves with red stems rise from deep-red, globular roots with consistently fine flesh. Introduced in 1892, it is a descendant of the popular Early Blood Turnip-Rooted Beet, which dates to 1820.

Early Wonder Tall-Top

Introduced in the U.S. in 1911, Early Wonder is a quick-growing, heavy producer that is a staple in many American gardens. Its abundant, dark-green, glossy leaves have a flavor that's prized for cooking. The somewhat squat roots are medium-red with flesh lightening toward the center.

Lutz Green Leaf

Also known as Winter Keeper, Lutz earned a reputation for keeping its flavor and crispness in the era before refrigeration. Along with being one of the best for fall harvest and winter storage, it has tops that grow quite tall—to 18 inches—without losing sweetness or becoming tough. Lighter green leaves have a pink blush on the ribs; the medium-red root is shaped like a spinning top.

BROCCOLI

Brassica oleracea
italica

One can practically *see* the nutrition present in the bunching florets of a head of broccoli, tightly gathered as though clutched in an invisible hand. It's *Brassica*'s bouquet—delivering the most showy, delectable vegetable in the Brassicaceae, or mustard family. Broccoli has also been found to contain cancer-fighting compounds as well as a generous supply of vitamins and minerals. But perhaps its best attribute is its variety of forms; in the supermarket you'll find that familiar bunched head, but in the garden you can cultivate plants with purple shoots of individual florets, or a yellow-green cauliflower-like head with amazing, multipointed fractal designs. All forms are quite easy to grow and produce a reliable crop, some coming in the early spring when the garden is otherwise producing only leafy greens.

Italy is broccoli's country of origin, where it was cultivated from wild strains growing in coastal regions, and today's varieties are still a great choice for a maritime climate. Brought to the U.S. by Italian immigrants in the 1800s, broccoli was far from an instant hit. Although mentioned in early gardening books, and listed in Thomas Jefferson's plantings at Monticello, it was not a popular catalog vegetable until the twentieth century. A duo of Italian brothers began growing it in California and shipping it to the burgeoning Italian immigrant population in Boston. Through their savvy promotion, it became a staple on American tables.

CULTIVATION   Because its seeds need warm soil (at least 70°F) to germinate, start it indoors and transplant out at five to six weeks, when the third or fourth set of leaves has formed. It may be planted out in early

spring for summer harvest, or in late summer/early fall for overwintering, which will provide a harvest in midspring.

Plant in fertile, well-worked soil, and side-dress with fertilizer
or compost during its growing season. To avoid soil-borne diseases,
rotate broccoli into a different garden bed each year. Also give suf-
ficient spacing between plants, 18 to 24 inches apart, as they do best
when sun is not blocked and can become rangy when crowded.

Purple Sprouting

HARVEST AND STORAGE

Cut broccoli heads when they are two-thirds grown, rather than seeking full size. Do not let the heads begin to loosen and show signs of flowering. When the head is cut, the plant begins to produce side shoots, which also should be cut when they still appear as tight florets. If broccoli's yellow flower petals begin to appear, the taste will be significantly more bitter.

Remarking that market broccoli can get stale and have "an intensely bitter flavor," the nineteenth-century French garden experts Messrs. Vilmorin-Andrieux wrote, "Every one who can should grow their own and cut it an hour before dinner!" If you need to store it after harvest, it will keep, unwashed and plastic-wrapped, in the refrigerator for a few days.

SEED SAVING

Broccoli is a biennial plant, but in mild climates it can produce a mature seed head in one season. If left in the garden for two years, plants can be dug and moved to the edge of a bed, where their rangy flower heads—which can get to be 4 feet tall—will be decorative but out of the way. To ensure genetic diversity, save seed from multiple plants if possible.

TIP

Succession planting is especially useful for heading broccoli, where one head can easily provide a dinner vegetable for two to three people. Plant three successions of seeds, two or three weeks apart, beginning in early spring. This will extend the harvest season by a month or more. If too much broccoli is ready at once, however, it does take pretty well to being blanched and bagged for the freezer.

VARIETIES

Calabrese

A large blue-green head develops first, followed by an abundance of tender side shoots, which can continue over a long harvest, especially in a cool climate. This variety is sometimes called Italian Green Sprouting.

A reliable broccoli that delivers blue-green mid-sized heads on a 24- to 36-inch plant. As heads are developing, young leaves can be cut and used like collard greens. After the central head is cut, side shoots will appear in two to three weeks. Good for a cool season, also for fall planting.

DeCiccio

An old European name for this attractive variety was "asparagus broccoli," because it does not form a central head but instead just sends out shoots, which are cut and eaten like asparagus. The florets and leaf tips have an attractive purple blush, but they turn uniformly green when cooked. This variety takes two-thirds of a year to produce, so plant after the heat of summer to begin eating in midspring.

Purple Sprouting

Certainly the most unique-looking brassica, Romanesco produces cauliflower-shaped heads that develop in an incredible fractal design, with many yellow-green tips in a whorled pattern. It's an amazing decorative plant, but some say it's also the most flavorful broccoli.

Romanesco

CABBAGE

Brassica oleracea

Cabbage is one of those vegetables that many gardeners skip over, but I think it deserves another look. Not only do the swelling, dense heads deliver a substantial crop with great nutritional properties, but they can be grown in mild areas through the winter and harvested when most of the garden is dormant. On top of that, if carefully stored, they keep well.

But don't rely only on the facts; once you eat a home-grown cabbage, your taste buds will do the deciding, as it is often much sweeter than store-bought. And if you grow a savoy cabbage, you'll congratulate yourself for also adding this strikingly handsome brassica to your landscape.

January King

Cabbage has been cultivated for thousands of years, and it is thought to have been a staple in Greek and Roman times. Northern Europeans developed many of the varieties we have today, which were brought to America by the colonists. Cabbage can appear in many cuisines—made into cole slaw, sauerkraut, or kim chee. In addition, it's a healthy addition to soups, stews, and stir-fries.

The common round cabbage found in the grocery store is the most recent type to be developed. Smaller, egg-shaped varieties, such as Early Jersey Wakefield, were cultivated for home gardening rather than market farming. The savoy, which gets its name from a region of southern France, is a looser-headed type that is also primarily for home use, since it is not a long keeper. It is, however, prized for a richer flavor and the unusual beauty of its blistered, netted leaves. According to *Winter Gardening in the Maritime Northwest* author Binda Colebrook, those deeply crenellated leaves may make it hardier in the garden.

CULTIVATION

Cabbage is grown like its brassica relative broccoli. It likes fertile, well-draining soil with a good layer of compost to hold in the moisture. Seeds need warm soil (70°F) to germinate, so it's best started indoors in cool climates, and planted out at five to seven weeks. It is a heavy feeder, so fertilize the bed when planting. Sow seeds 6 inches apart, but thin to 24 inches. Regular water is a must for good head development and a healthy plant; inconsistent water can cause the heads to split.

Heads develop in cool weather, so plant shorter-season varieties in spring to harvest midsummer, and longer-season ones in late summer to eat during the winter or let stand in the garden until spring. Plants grown for summer harvest tend to become strong-tasting or bolt when hot weather hits, and a root rot can develop.

HARVEST AND STORAGE
: Prompt harvest is critical for early-season varieties, which can split easily if they over-ripen. Fall-planted cabbage will develop more slowly and can be left to stand in the garden much longer without detriment. Harvest by cutting the head an inch or so above the base of the stem, including a few of the outer wrapper leaves. If not used promptly, it will store for up to two months in a moist, cool place in newspaper or sawdust.

SEED SAVING
: Saving your own cabbage seed is a two-year proposition because this biennial sends up a seed stalk in its second year. Because the plant crosses easily with others of the *B. oleracea* species, including broccoli and cauliflower, you must be careful not to save seed of multiple varieties without giving them significant physical distance. In a home garden, perhaps just save one of this species each year.

TIP
: Many people think savoy cabbages are the tastiest varieties, but they have tougher, more heavily webbed leaves, which means they will take longer to cook. As the head is developing, however, you can cut individual leaves and use them as you would collards.

VARIETIES

Early Jersey Wakefield
: Early American gardeners didn't have much luck with the popular English variety Early Wakefield, so a New Jersey truck farmer developed his own. It went on to be acquired by seedsman Peter Henderson in the 1860s and became the most popular cabbage on the market for many years. It has an egg-shaped, 5-inch head that can reach three pounds. Its small size allows closer spacing, perhaps 18 inches apart. Outer leaves are dark green with white ribs and have a waxy finish; inner leaves are crisp and finely textured. It has a mild, sweet flavor, the core is smaller than most, and it is resistant to splitting.

This semi-savoy has slightly flattened, looser, relatively small heads. The light-green leaves, darkening toward the edges, attain red to purple colorations on the tips and outer blistered leaves, especially after a cold snap. It is fascinating to watch the color develop as the head grows. It is very hardy—some think it the best winter cabbage—but it can use protection from a harsh winter. Its flavor mellows after a frost, and it keeps well. A variety prized in England, it is not as commonly found in the U.S.

January King

CARROTS

Daucus carota

Children love carrots, and are especially delighted when they can pull them straight from the ground. The look on many a young face will say "Amazing!" Indeed, the popular vegetable earns that label: it's easy to grow in the right soil, high in nutrients, and wonderful to eat. And carrots aren't just for children, or for that matter, even just for humans. They're a sweet treat for horses, and one gardening friend even lost her entire crop one year to her dog, who dug them up and devoured them on the spot.

Heirloom carrots conjure up amazement, too, when you consider that carrots originated in the wilds of Afghanistan, where early ones had purple or nearly black roots with yellow flesh and were not eaten. Early carrots also could be red, yellow, white, or even green. When first cultivated in Europe (they were a favorite vegetable of England's Queen Elizabeth I), carrots were mostly yellow, until the famous French horticulturalist Henry Vilmorin crossed a pale yellow carrot with its wild relative, the common meadow flower Queen Anne's lace, and came up with a white carrot. Perhaps they've come full circle, because today you can find carrots of many hues, but the most popular are still orange and red.

Some of today's favorite heirlooms are named after their places of origin, from small French towns like Nantes, an area where a number of sweet, tapered varieties were developed, to the New England hamlet of Danvers, Massachusetts, which became famous for its sturdy, reliable variety.

CULTIVATION   Carrots are always grown *in situ* from seeds. Their single taproot wants to grow straight into the earth, so they require a loose, sandy soil with few stones. Turn the bed and add compost prior to planting if the soil is compacted or has a heavier clay element. (Don't enrich it with manure or a fertilizer high in nitrogen, though, or the roots will get excessively hairy and fork or split.) The "double-digging" technique (see Sidebar) is especially useful to create an excellent carrot bed. For full root development, loosen the soil down to 10 inches. If the soil is heavy, carrots will be stunted or their roots will fork. An exception is the heirloom Oxheart, a stubby variety that will force its way through denser dirt.

To spread the tiny carrot seed evenly, mix it with a bit of sand and sprinkle it in shallow furrows. Thin to 1–3 inches apart, depending on variety. Sow in succession every two to three weeks from spring to midsummer, and you will be harvesting carrots into early winter. In moderate climates (or if you use a cold frame or cloche), a fall sowing can be made, so you will have an early spring crop. A winter carrot crop can be the sweetest and crispest of the year.

A floating row cover of spun polyester material can be used to cover the bed after planting. This will help retain moisture, increase the soil temperature and, most important, prevent the carrot rust fly from laying its eggs at the base of the plant. The rust fly larvae burrow into the carrot, leaving black woody tracks or tunnels that can ruin the root. Cover the bed loosely with row cover, and cover the edges of the material with soil to hold it down.

Keep the soil evenly moist during the seeds' long germination time, which may be two to three weeks. When the carrots are the width of a pencil, thin the plants to the correct spacing given on the seed packet to ensure that the roots will develop to full size. Keep the bed well weeded.

Danvers Half Long

HARVEST AND STORAGE

Carrots are ready to harvest when their color is brightest and roots are formed to the specified length for each variety. The tops should be glossy green and bushy. Begin pulling one carrot of each type as the variety's maturity date approaches. If the flesh becomes woody or the carrots crack, they have gone too long. To store or over-winter in the ground, mulch carrots with 2 to 3 inches of loose material such as straw or leaves. You can also pull them, break off the tops, and store them in damp sand in a protected dark place, or refrigerate them in a loose plastic bag for two to three weeks.

SEED SAVING

Carrots are biennial, so the seed specimens need to be left in the ground a year before going to seed. Then they will produce an umbel—a spray of flower stems that resemble the spines of an umbrella. (These striking flower stalks can be left in the garden to dry, or can be cut and air-dried.) If the weed Queen Anne's lace grows in your area, it will very likely cross with the carrot flowers through insect pollination, making seed saving useless. When harvesting seed, shake it through a fine screen. This will remove the chaff, and also partially "debeard" the seed of its hairy covering.

TIP Although carrots are very often eaten raw, that is not their most nutritious form. Because our digestive system cannot fully process the fibrous carrot cells, a greater level of the antioxidant carotene can be gained from cooked carrots, and the percentage is even higher in carrot juice.

VARIETIES

Danvers Half Long This variety entered American kitchen gardens in the early 1870s, developed by farmers near Danvers, Massachusetts. It is a good choice for shorter growing seasons and will produce in heavier soils. Roots are 6 to 8 inches, tapered, and bright orange.

Oxheart Also known as Guérande and from Nantes, this stout variety was developed in the 1870s. It grows to 6 inches long and perhaps 4 inches wide, and tapers to a blunt end. Not as sweet as some varieties, but this thick, pale orange carrot is great for cooking. Roots can be up to a pound each, and keep well.

Red-Cored Chantenay The striking red center of the Chantenay makes it attractive when sliced, and its ability to grow in heavier soil makes it desirable too. Roots are 5 to 7 inches long and almost cylindrical, with a slight taper. The fine-grained, crisp flesh has a pleasant sweetness that increases in storage.

An orange, cylindrical carrot with a hint of red in the flesh, Scarlet Nantes is popular not only with home gardeners but with market farmers as well, due to its excellent production and good flavor for eating fresh. It has a smooth skin, yellow to orange flesh, and a mild, small core.

Scarlet Nantes

Another Nantes variety, similar to Scarlet Nantes except for its color, which tends toward orange rather than red. Crisp, fine flesh on 6-inch tapered roots; wonderful for fresh eating.

Touchon

DOUBLE DIGGING

This technique, in which you excavate your garden bed and then fill it in again, could be considered prison labor, but in fact it's quite a productive activity for a garden with heavy soil. It is especially good for root crops such as carrots that need a deep, loose bed of soil to develop, or for beds that have been left fallow for some time and become compacted. However, do not double dig the same bed year after year, as that reduces the soil's tilth.

1. *Stake out a rectangular bed, clearing vegetation.*
2. *Using a flat-bladed shovel, cut a trench one shovel-head deep across the bed, depositing the soil in a mound on the far side.*
3. *Use a garden fork to loosen the soil at the bottom of the trench.*
4. *Add 1 to 2 inches of compost to the trench, mixing it into the loosened soil. If the soil is very dense, a layer of sand can also be added.*
5. *Dig another trench next to the first, depositing the soil into the first trench. Continue this process down the bed.*
6. *When the last trench has been dug and soil loosened, deposit soil from the first trench into it.*
7. *Add a top layer of compost and fertilizer to the soil, digging it a few inches into the raised bed.*

CHARD

Beta vulgaris

The broad, upright ribs and leaves of chard, also known as Swiss chard, "silver beet," or "spinach beet," stand like sentinels in the garden, at attention throughout their lives. The plant is a member of the beet genus, *Beta*, sharing many of the beet's characteristics but lacking its swollen root. Chard originated in the south of Europe and was a popular vegetable among the Greeks, even earning a mention in Aristotle's writings. One of the most delightful varieties, Rainbow chard, was lost for many years to home gardeners but, thanks to the efforts of Seed Savers Exchange, has become pretty widely available again in seed catalogs.

Rainbow

Especially attractive to me are chard's smooth, brightly colored ribs and stems (which horticulturalist Fearing Burr Jr. in the 1860s called "nerves," a biologically interesting term). The stems are flat and can be quite broad, setting off nicely the richly colored leaves. The leaves can be smooth or quite savoyed, and can be a foot in length and half as broad. The juicy stems are chopped and used in stir-fries, soups, or egg dishes; the leaves, prepared like beet greens, are wonderful and very nutritious, although they have a more earthy flavor, like spinach. If you are cooking both together, strip the greens off the stems, chop the stems, and begin their cooking first, adding the leaves when the stems have softened.

CULTIVATION Grow in place, from seed. Plant in fertile, loose soil, and provide regular water when young, after which the plants will largely thrive on their own. Germinating in soil as cool as 50°F, chard can be one of the earlier vegetables planted in the spring. In a mild climate, one planting can yield a nearly perpetual crop, but you can use succession sowing if you want to extend the harvest. You also can sow in July for an overwintering crop.

When plants are 3 inches high, thin to 8 to 12 inches apart. Side-dress with a balanced fertilizer when plants are 6 inches tall. Don't use a nitrogen-heavy fertilizer, as the faster leaf growth can compromise the flavor.

HARVEST AND STORAGE Snap or clip off outer leaves; the rosette-shaped plant sends new leaves from its center. Trim off any leaves that have been windowpaned by slugs or leaf miners. Regular harvesting of leaves encourages growth. Chard is best if used immediately, but can be stored unwashed in plastic for most of a week.

SEED SAVING Chard is a biennial, sending up a seed stalk in its second year. It crosses easily with beets and other chard varieties, so isolation is necessary to get true seed. Pot up seed plants to overwinter in a warmer area if necessary, or move to the edge of the garden to let it go to seed.

TIP Chard makes a wonderful ornamental plant, offering up its cheery brightness quite nicely along a border. Try this for next winter: Choose a flowerbed that has good visibility from your house, and grow a spring cutting flower there—something you won't mind pulling out by midsummer. Then sow a thick, undulating row of Rainbow chard in its place. You'll be guaranteed a splash of color through winter that stands up to cold—and stands out even more after a light snow.

VARIETIES

Fordhook Giant This popular variety has been around since 1750. It produces large, very vigorous plants, with deeply crinkled dark green leaves; broad white ribs and stems; and juicy, celerylike stalks. Its heavy production and good flavor make it one of the most commonly grown chards.

Golden A medium-sized variety with stems that start yellow and deepen to gold. Leaves are medium to dark green, smooth, and flat. Mild and sweet.

Rainbow Also called Five-Colored Silver Beet, this plant delights gardeners with stem colors of white, pink, red, orange, and yellow, and leaf colors from light to dark green to nearly purple. Its leaves are not as heavily savoyed as those of other chards.

Rhubarb Also known as Ruby Red, it was introduced in 1857. Deep crimson, thick and fleshy stalks and veins hold up nearly black-green leaves that are very crinkled. The mildest-tasting chard. It is shorter than some varieties, and very ornamental.

CORN

Zea mays

Corn is as basic a staple as can be found in the garden, but its overuse as a commercial crop has made it much maligned among people who value biodiversity for personal and ecosystem health. However, just because it has become the monocrop of choice for everything from sugars to biofuels, it should not be shunned from the home garden. In fact, it should be revered as the historic, valuable, and versatile plant that it is.

An ancient crop, corn originated in Mexico. For centuries, it's been an essential staple for native peoples throughout the Americas. Native Americans grew many different kinds of corn in an amazing array of colors and types, and it has been valuable in their spiritual practices as well.

There are five kinds of corn: flint, flour, dent, sweet, and popcorn. The first three are dried for flour or to reconstitute in soups; the last one is for the movies; but it's sweet corn that's the prime object of our affection. For some people, sinking their teeth into a hot, juicy ear of freshly roasted corn is the pinnacle of summer eating. Such is the fervor that people clamor for it when it's fresh—one old variety was named Howling Mob by its breeder because that's what he experienced when he took it to market— and opine strongly about how it should be prepared. The author Russell Baker once described the perfect way to harvest and cook corn. First, get a pot of water boiling. Then strip the ears off the stalks, strip off the husks, and run for the house to plunge the ears instantly into the water, just barely scalding them to bring out the sweet flavor.

I'm not a howling corn fanatic, but I do enjoy a toothsome ear at summer barbecues, and I like to try to grow it on occasion.

Golden Bantam

The short season of a maritime garden means it's best to choose varieties that don't get Iowa tall or put out super-sized ears. With heirloom corn varieties, a gardener finds unique choices that are not as sweet as today's hybrid sweet corn (witness categories that breeders have named Sugar Enhanced, Supersweet, and Triplesweet), but possibly have a finer or more pronounced corn taste. And as with most heirlooms, you'll be regrowing the story behind the variety as well as the vegetable itself. Be sure to share its history when tonging the steaming ear onto your picnic guest's plate.

CULTIVATION

Soil temperature will be the most critical element of getting corn off to a good start in a cooler, shorter maritime growing season. Soil temperature at planting time must be at least 60 to 65°F, or the sugars in the dried kernels will quickly cause them to rot. Two solutions: warm the soil with a floating row cover or another season extender, or start the plants indoors. If using a row cover, cover the bed for weeks prior to planting to pre-warm the soil, and then leave the cover on the bed until the plants are a few inches high. Use a soil thermometer to ensure it's in the right range. If starting the seeds indoors, plan the germination and growing time so that by planting-out time—which is when the plants are 3 to 6 inches high, before the taproot really begins to develop—the weather will be predictably warm.

Corn needs to be planted in squares for proper pollination. Instead of one long row, plot out at least four short rows, 2 feet apart. Another traditional way is to plant a hill of seeds fairly close together, and thin to four stalks: "One for the mouse, one for the crow, one to rot, and one to grow." When thinned, the corn plants should be 8 to 12 inches apart. Plant in a sunny spot—and pay attention to what the plants will be shading when they reach their full height of 5 or 6 feet. When corn is knee high (by the Fourth of July, if you're lucky...), fertilize with alfalfa meal, which provides a slow release of nitrogen. Keep the plants well watered, and increase the water when the tassels emerge from the stalk, which will aid in kernel development. Expect to get two ears per stalk.

Critters can be a problem with corn at both planting and harvest stages. A floating row cover can prevent crows from pulling your seeds out of the soil. As the corn matures, squirrels and raccoons crave the kernels. Although it's not a perfect defense, you can deter them by caging each ear in a sleeve made of quarter-inch wire mesh, secured beyond each end of the ear.

HARVEST AND STORAGE

Corn is ready to harvest for fresh eating when a milky juice squirts out of a kernel that you puncture with your thumbnail. This is called the milk stage, and it's when sweet corn is eaten. Because the sugars in corn turn to starch fairly quickly—and this is especially true with heirloom corn—it should be eaten quickly after harvest.

For types that are eaten dried, such as popcorn, it is best to dry the cobs on the stalk. Husk them, and continue to dry them in a warm place out of the sun until kernels twist fairly easily from the cob. If you have a lot of corn to husk, pile it on a tarp, don some stout, clean boots, and stomp the kernels off. Store the kernels in an airtight container; popcorn is best if it's stored for up to a year before using.

SEED SAVING Saving corn seed is not a realistic option for home gardeners. Too many plants would have to be saved for selection in order for the seed to not get weak from inbreeding. Corn saved and replanted from a small quantity at home will likely not be very vigorous.

TIP You don't have to pull back the husk on an ear of corn to see its ripeness if you use this visual test: When the white or yellow silk turns brown and starts to dry, the corn is ripe.

VARIETIES

Black Aztec Also known as Black Mexican, Mexican Sweet, and Black Iroquois. The last name probably hits closest to its origin, as it is thought to have been developed in upstate New York, rather than being an old variety from the Aztecs. Although it's been grown for hundreds of years, it was introduced to the seed trade in the 1860s. The ears are good for fresh eating when the kernels are still white, but as the milk stage progresses, they turn purple and then bluish black. Plants are modestly sized at 5 to 6 feet, with ears 7 to 8 inches long. The dark kernels are very hard when dried, but can be ground for blue cornmeal.

Golden Bantam A sweet corn that is also called Golden Bantam 8 Row. It was developed by J. G. Pickett near Greenfield, Massachusetts, and introduced to gardeners by W. Atlee Burpee in 1902. Before Golden Bantam, people did not eat yellow-kerneled sweet corn— it was "horse feed." But Bantam delivers the essence of fresh corn with a wonderful, lightly sweet flavor in plump kernels. Also, it is ready for harvest ten to fifteen days earlier than other popular open-pollinated sweet corn. It is not as sugary as hybrids, and must be picked and eaten promptly because the milk stage is short. Plants are 5 to 6 feet tall, ears are 5 to 7 inches long. May be grown more closely than some varieties.

This much-loved sweet corn has set the standard for heirloom corn. Named after its breeder, Nathan Stowell, who developed it in New Jersey in 1848, it is called Evergreen because it remains in the milk stage longer than many varieties. Growers used to harvest it by pulling the entire plant and hanging it upside down in a cool place, where the ears would last into the winter. Plants can reach 10 feet, with large 8- to 9-inch ears with eighteen rows of kernels. Needs a longer growing season, up to 100 days.

Stowell's Evergreen

Squat, 2-inch ears of burgundy kernels are extremely decorative, but the kernels can be taken off the husk and popped to yield a wonderful small white popcorn. Grows up to four ears on a stalk that is under 5 feet tall. Also known as Dwarf Strawberry.

Strawberry

CORN SALAD

Valerianella locusta

Also known as mâche, lamb's lettuce, or its very old name fetticus, this delicate yet hardy gourmet salad green has a long history in the maritime garden. It comes from Europe, and until the mid-1800s was mainly growing wild and simply collected from the fields. It is unrelated to *Zea mays;* its name derives from the fact that in England it grew among fields of wheat, which is known there as "corn."

Corn salad grows in a rosette, and often the entire plant is used once it's mature, although individual leaves can be picked while it's sizing up. It grows best in cooler climates, so it's perfect as a year-round green for the maritime garden. Use it raw in salads as a counterpoint to the more spicy arugula or mustards, or on its own as a refreshing light garnish to meats or hearty winter stews.

CULTIVATION Corn salad is not a fussy grower and will do well under many conditions, but it's best in well-cultivated loam, in climates with daytime
temperatures up to 75°F. Plant it in early spring and practice suc-
cession-sowing every two weeks to have a supply of corn salad well
into summer. With another planting in the fall in temperate areas,
you can enjoy it again in late winter. Use a balanced fertilizer when
planting. Sow heavily, and thin plants to 6 inches apart.

It is very cold tolerant and does not generally need winter
cover unless prolonged cold and snow are predicted. In my garden
it has somewhat naturalized, and I regularly find succulent young
corn salad leaves among the arugula and chard.

HARVEST AND Clip off the entire plant when it has reached expected size, with
STORAGE leaves 2 to 3 inches long and the plant up to 8 inches across, or cut
individual leaves as it grows. It doesn't store well, so wash and use
it immediately after harvesting.

D'Etampes

Corn salad will readily go to seed. The seed heads may be harvested and dried in paper bags; then the seed can be shaken out and stored.

To enhance its nutty taste, use a light nut oil as a salad dressing.

VARIETY

Also known as Verte d'Etampes, this variety has a darker green leaf with more pronounced veining than the lighter Italian varieties. It grows close to the ground on a compact rosette. Its leaves are slightly more firm than those of other varieties, so it holds up better in use.

D'Etampes

ENDIVE

Chicorium endivia

Endive, a member of the chicory genus, offers a distinctive bitter flavor. Although the chicories are many and varied, two heirloom endives that provide a nice counterpoint when mixed lightly into salads or sautés are the French type frisée, a lighter, wispy member of the endive clan, and the broad-leaf variety commonly known as escarole. Although we see it as a European plant, broad-leaved endive is thought to have originated in Egypt centuries ago.

A related chicory, *C. intybus,* the upright Belgian endive, whose leaves are often blanched and used to carry spreads in hors d'oeuvres, is not included in this book.

Frisée produces a mound of pale, slightly nutty-tasting leaves that can be trimmed over a long season. It's a beautiful plant, whose light green frills rise from a pure white center. Escarole produces a

Très Fine Maraîchère

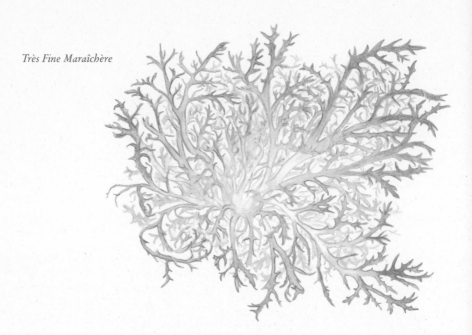

loose head of sturdy, darker green leaves growing thickly around a pale yellow center.

CULTIVATION Sow in late spring for a plant that will produce leaves in the maritime climate for much of the summer. It also may be started indoors and planted on the same schedule as lettuce. It can be sown again in fall and overwintered in mild climates with protection under a cloche. Prepare the seedbed as for any green, digging in a balanced fertilizer prior to planting. Keep well watered during germination, after which it should require little effort. Thin to 10 inches apart.

HARVEST AND Frisée is excellent as a cut-and-come-again green. Pinch off indi-
STORAGE vidual leaves that have reached 4 to 6 inches in length, or trim the

whole plant with scissors down to 1 inch above the soil. Frisée does not keep well and should be used immediately after harvest. Individual leaves of escarole, which stands up better to refrigeration, may be eaten raw when small, but when sized for harvest are best when cooked.

Plants of *C. endivia* are biennial, so they must be left for a second year to flower and go to seed, unless they bolt during the first season due to weather conditions. The tall flower stalks will produce numerous seed heads, which may be left to dry on the plant. Test for maturity by pinching off a lower one when visibly dry and shelling it. The seed should be dark, hard, and dry. Dried pods can be stored and planted whole, or broken open at planting time.

SEED SAVING

Some people like to blanch endive prior to harvest to make it milder and less bitter. About a week before harvesting, gather up the leaves and bundle them with a rubber band or string, or cover the entire plant with an overturned pot.

TIP

VARIETIES

Commonly known as escarole, this endive dates to 1934. It has a loosely formed round head that can reach 12 inches, with lettuce-like outer leaves. It's wonderful grilled, or may be used in salads, soups, and stews.

Broad-Leaved Batavian

This small, quick-growing frisée can reach 8 inches in diameter, with finely cut leaves 4 to 6 inches long. It is said to have originated in France in the nineteenth century. Much sweeter and milder than large-leaf endive, it can be used in small quantities to add a touch of bitter spice to salads.

Très Fine Maraîchère

GARLIC

Allium sativum

Each July, I carefully pry the garlic bulbs from the warm earth of my summer garden, soil clinging to their roots. At the end of each drying stalk, the bulb swells with a dozen plump cloves. The purple haze of my favorite variety, Spanish Roja, can be seen through the silvery skin like a sunrise appearing through the clouds. The colorful streaks of this Northwest heirloom signal a bit of spice or heat, much more so than the white supermarket offering. Garlic reaches its peak of flavor after curing. Used fresh, it has a very green, tangy flavor, while cured garlic is more mellow or more spicy, depending on the variety.

The many varieties of garlic fall into two categories, softneck and hardneck. The softneck ones are generally milder and produce cloves in multiple layers. Their stems will flop over when they're ripe, and the plants can be braided after harvest. Hardnecks can be very spicy, and you monitor their ripeness by the drying of the leaves. They generally produce one layer of cloves around the central stem. Within these two categories are various subcategories, such as Artichoke (so named because the cloves are layered like artichoke leaves), Rocambole, Purple Stripe, Creole, Porcelain, Silverskin, and Asiatic. With all the varieties in so many categories, it could be a lifelong undertaking to try a new garlic or two each year.

As I tie bunches of the garlic together with twine to cure by hanging in my garage, I pull out some of the larger heads and group them together. These will be my "seed," to be saved for fall planting of next year's crop. In a decade of saving and replanting my own garlic, I've probably saved a couple of hundred dollars in seed garlic (and maintained my favorite variety, which is not always easily found commercially). But, more important, I've closed the loop on my use of garlic—a staple in our kitchen—and that is deeply satisfying.

The great California garlic grower Chester Aaron wrote "Garlic is life" in his delightful book of the same name. If so, I've brought life to my soil and to many hundreds of meals, as my garlic has spiced up countless dishes made of other home-grown vegetables.

CULTIVATION

Plant as the autumn leaves are falling, and harvest when the tomatoes are ripening. In Seattle, I plant my garlic in the last half of October; in warmer areas, it could be planted into November.

Garlic is grown by planting individual cloves split from a healthy head. Separate the head and plant only the largest, plumpest cloves with the papery skin intact. Plant the cloves 6 to 8 inches apart in rows 8 to 12 inches apart, pointed end up and flat end down, in well-draining soil. The tip of the clove should be 2 inches or so beneath the surface. Cover the soil with up to 4 inches of loose mulch like straw or shredded leaves to keep the bed warmer and reduce weeds.

Spanish Roja

First shoots appear in early winter in the maritime climate, or later if winter is unusually harsh. Garlic loves a fertile, loose soil and does not compete well with weeds. Fertilize by side-dressing with a dry, balanced organic blend once in early spring, and then at least once more in late spring. Keep the bed weeded and watered evenly during spring and early summer, discontinuing supplemental water a month prior to harvest.

HARVEST AND STORAGE

Harvest when the bottom two sets of leaves are brown and drying. Do not pull the plants from the ground—use a garden fork or spade and unearth the entire plant, keeping the tops attached.

Because different varieties mature at different rates, dig one plant up to test for harvest timing; cloves should be full and firm to the touch, covered in a sturdy, papery skin. On overripe garlic, cloves will separate and may soften or shrivel.

To cure, shake off loose soil and trim the roots to within a half-inch of the bulb. Hang upside down in a dry place out of the sun, such as a shed or garage, with good air circulation. Softneck varieties can be braided, while others can be hung by twine individually or in small groups. After three to four weeks, the garlic can be taken down and cleaned up for storage. Clip off the stems to 1 inch above the head, trim the roots very closely, and lightly brush off any outer wrapper layers that are encrusted with dirt, taking care not to completely unwrap the cloves. Then tag the garlic by variety, and store it in mesh onion bags or some other breathable packaging such as paper bags or wicker baskets. Keep in a cool, dry place with low light. Storage time depends upon variety, but many will keep three to six months or longer.

SEED SAVING   Home gardeners often select the best heads of their current crop as seed garlic for next year's planting, and new gardeners could seek a starter head or two from gardening friends. The variety sold in supermarkets is often neither unique nor desirable for home cultivation, but farmers market growers are keeping great varieties in circulation. To save a head for seed, follow the curing procedure above; then label its variety and store separately from your cooking garlic until planting time.

TIP   In early spring, cut the curly flowering top of the garlic plant (known as the "scape") to trigger the underground bulb to develop its cloves. Not all varieties produce scapes, but when the green shoots appear, they make a fresh springtime treat when steamed or stir-fried. The scapes of some varieties produce a cluster of "bulbils" at their tips, which can be harvested, dried, and planted as seed, but doing so will often produce smaller garlic than the clove-planting method.

VARIETIES

A Porcelain style that has five to eight very fat cloves per head. Porcelains do not provide as much seed garlic as the many-cloved varieties, but they have become prized for their flavors when raw. Georgian Fire comes from the Republic of Georgia, the place of origin for many well-loved varieties. It is a spicy garlic that Washington specialty grower Filaree Farm recommends for salsa and salads.

Georgian Fire

First discovered on the Colville Indian reservation in Eastern Washington, this mild garlic regularly wins taste prizes. An Artichoke variety, it has large heads and softneck stems, and keeps well up to nine months.

Inchelium Red

A marbled Purple Stripe variety that grower Bob Anderson calls "Great Bulbs of Fire," Metechi produces an amazingly large head on a handsome, vigorous plant with large bulbils developing on its curled scape. It's one of the larger and later-maturing varieties. The cloves will be few in number but large, elongated, and crescent-shaped, with sturdy white bulb wrappers that reveal purple when peeled. It's fiery hot when raw, flavorful in cooking. It will store longer than many varieties.

Metechi

Discovered in the San Juan Islands of Washington State, this strong-flavored heirloom is now widely grown. With eighteen to twenty-four cloves in a pure white bulb, this Silverskin softneck variety is beautiful braided and a stellar variety to store and use all winter.

Nootka Rose

Oregon Blue | A high-producing Northwest heirloom with a fairly hot flavor. An Artichoke strain, it has large bulbs on a vigorous plant. It has a soft-neck top, produces eight to ten cloves, and is good for storage.

Spanish Roja | A more spicy variety, it was brought to the Portland, Oregon, area before the 1900s and is also called Greek or Greek Blue. It is wonderful with stir-fry vegetables or slipped under the skin of a roast chicken. This hardneck Rocambole variety, with thinner skins and a pale pink clove edge, is a shorter keeper.

KALE & COLLARDS

Brassica oleracea

Although quite different in appearance, both kale and collards are stewing greens that are quite hardy and rich in vitamins. They're very easy to grow and do well in a cool maritime climate, where they can produce heavily during warmer weather and continue to thrive through fall and winter. They actually become sweeter after being hit by frost.

Kale and collards are close relatives, members of the huge *Brassica* genus that includes broccoli, cabbage, kohlrabi, Brussels sprouts, Chinese cabbage, and mustards. Collards used to be called "colewort," and the name "kale" is also derived from the root *col-*, revealing why brassicas are often called "cole crops."

There are basically two types of kale: one with heavily curled leaves on an upright stalk, the other growing in a more open, broad-leaved manner. Collards generally grow as a collection of loose, open-headed leaves.

Both plants are great for soups or stewed with potatoes, or for a dish of "pot greens" with garlic, onion, and cooking stock. The sturdy, slightly bitter greens also stand well next to meat. Colonial Williamsburg's garden historian Wesley Green says that "beef and greens" was a dish found in Colonial diaries and that by "greens" the European settlers meant kale.

CULTIVATION

These brassicas take well to transplanting, so spring sowings may be started indoors and transplanted out after six weeks. They may also be direct-sown in midspring, after the soil has warmed somewhat. They need a soil temperature of 55 to 75°F to germinate. Avoid planting in the heat of summer, but plant again in late summer for an overwintering crop. Keep the soil moist throughout their growing season, especially through warm weather. Thin to 12 inches in rows 2 feet apart, or on 18-inch centers. Apply a balanced fertilizer after thinning.

Lacinato kale

HARVEST AND STORAGE

For kale, harvest outer leaves, and strip off any that have become too old, as they will be tough. Kale will refrigerate for a few days if necessary but should be chilled quickly to avoid wilting. If the plant is left to flower, the flowers and shoots are also quite tender and delicious.

For collards, use the more tender inner leaves but not the bunching center ones, and leave a ring of the largest outer leaves as well.

SEED SAVING

Like other brassicas, kale and collards are biennial, so they must be overwintered to produce seed in their second year. In a hard-winter climate, lift the plant and store in an above-freezing location. They are bee-pollinated, and will cross with other brassicas of their species, so the home gardener, for whom separating varieties by a half-mile is hardly a practical option, must leave only one variety to go to seed.

TIP

Remember that kale and collards are both brassicas—a key consideration of garden layout and succession planting. To control the insects and diseases that are common in the large cabbage family (which contains a variety of popular veggies, from broccoli to mustard), do not plant kale or collards in the same bed where you've just removed another brassica.

VARIETIES

Lacinato kale

Also known as Palm Tree, Black Tuscan Palm, and Dinosaur, this Italian heirloom dates from the eighteenth century. It has narrow, dark grey-green leaves with a chewy texture and mild flavor. The very heavily savoyed, blistered leaves curl under. When leaves are harvested from the bottom of the stem, as is standard practice, the upright plant resembles a palm tree later in the season. Leaves are 2 to 3 inches wide and can reach 2 feet in length on a plant 2 to 3 feet tall. Discard the rigid center rib before cooking.

An 1885 import that came via Canada, introduced there by French traders. Also called Ragged Jack, it has flat, open, blue-green leaves with a reddish tinge, resembling oak leaves but with ruffled edges, on a 2-foot plant. Stems are red to purple; in extreme cold they turn entirely red. The leaves are very tender. Use immediately upon picking. Also called Canadian broccoli because it puts out flower buds in early spring.

Russian Red kale

Heavy-producing plant up to 2 feet tall with leaves loosely forming a head. Smooth leaves are dark green, with light-green veins and undulating edges. Morris Heading is smaller than the common varieties grown in the southern U.S., such as Green Glaze and Georgia Green. The leaves are juicy and tender, with a mild flavor. The plant is hardy and slow to bolt.

Morris Heading collards

LEEKS

A well-rounded home vegetable garden must contain at least one—and ideally several—choices from the flavorful *Allium* genus, which includes onions, garlic, shallots, and leeks. Each member of this large genus contributes an aromatic freshness and a basic spice to many of our common dishes, and alliums are found in ethnic cooking from lands around the globe. The leek has a milder, more refined taste than the onion, and more substance and sweetness than garlic or shallots.

Allium ampeloprasum

I think of leeks as giving me a very serviceable onion substitute in winter. Whereas most onions, in a maritime climate, need to be pulled from the ground and used or stored in fall, leeks are just getting going, and can take over the onion's role of providing the pungent, sizzling base to winter soups and other vegetable dishes. What's more, the flavor of the leek, as with many winter-hardy vegetables, can improve after frost, and the plant can even withstand a freeze. If the cold does damage it, it often will just get back to business and regrow when mild weather reappears.

The leek dates back to very early civilizations, being found in Egyptian ruins, in the writings of the Romans, and in French and English recipes going back many centuries. Probably originating in the Mediterranean, it moved north over the years, and was quite beloved as a cool-season crop in the countries that are now the British Isles. In fact, the image of the leek—a fan shape of flat leaves on a broad central stalk—has long been a symbol of Wales.

Blue Solaise

Stories are told of Welsh soldiers wearing leeks in their helmets to identify them on the battlefield, and such an identification was referred to in Shakespeare's play *Henry V*.

Grow leeks in loose, fertile soil that has been amended with compost or manure; they do not respond as well to heavy soil. They need to be well watered throughout the growing season. A cool-season crop, they can be set out in the garden in early spring in a mild climate for harvest by midsummer, but they're best planted to overwinter, which means setting them out after the heat of summer has passed.

Sowing seed directly into the garden is possible, but with the shorter warm seasons of a maritime climate, better results come from starting leeks indoors and planting them out. They are slow in coming to maturity, so start the seeds nearly three months before your target planting date. The goal is to get the plants to size up considerably before winter hits. Plants should ultimately be 4 to 5 inches apart, in rows 12 to 18 inches apart; when you thin them, use the small ones like scallions.

Because of their long season, make maximum use of your garden real estate by interplanting them with small root crops like radishes or leafy greens like lettuce. A row of lettuce between leek rows can come and go before the leeks have sized up.

CULTIVATION

Dig and use leeks whenever they're above one-half inch in diameter. When they are fully sized, they can remain in the ground for storage until needed. To clean leeks for use, split lengthwise and wash thoroughly, as they are notorious for harboring sandy soil in their tight rings.

HARVEST AND STORAGE

Leeks are biennial, so seed saving will happen in the second year. They can be lifted and put to the edge of the garden, and will need

SEED SAVING

support when the heavy head of seeds appears on a long flower stalk. They will cross-pollinate with other leek varieties, but not with other onions. Shake the hard, black seed from the drying stalks, which may be pulled and hung to finish the drying process if necessary.

TIP   The white lower part of the leek stalk is most desired in the kitchen, so maximizing that blanched section of stem will increase your yield. To blanch the stem, you can either plant young leeks in a trench about 6 inches deep, slowly filling the trench with more soil as they grow, or plant them at ground level and then mulch around their bases with compost as they grow. With either method, back-fill soil or compost carefully to get as little as possible into the leaf stems; this will make for easier cleaning in the kitchen.

VARIETIES

Blue Solaise   A beautiful heirloom from France (there called Bleu de Solaize) with broad, blue-green leaves that get violet-tinged edges when cold temperatures hit. The plant may appear to shiver (actually, the chlorophyll is draining away to reveal other colors), but it will perform just fine in the cold, holding well over the winter and putting on some growth during mild spurts. Maturing ten to thirty days earlier than some varieties, it is recommended for short seasons.

Giant Carentan   The 1885 book *The Vegetable Garden* by Messrs. Vilmorin-Andrieux describes this variety, but it was called Giant Italian when introduced to the U.S. at about that time. It has 8-inch-long, dark-green leaves on stalks easily 3 inches in diameter or greater, and is vigorous and fast growing. It is sensitive to drought and heat and needs a longer season, but does well when overwintered.

This leek is also known as American Flag or Scottish Flag, but not because soldiers waved it in battles. Rather, "flag" refers to the fan-shaped leaves. It was developed by seed growers near Musselburgh, now a suburb of Edinburgh, from a variety called London Flag. Having originated on the Scottish coast, it is well adapted to maritime climates. It has a paler green leaf than most leeks, and a smooth stalk of 2 to 3 inches in diameter with length up to 15 inches, which is where it got its "giant" designation. Territorial Seed Company reports that Musselburgh was the slowest leek to bolt in its Oregon trial gardens.

Giant Musselburgh

LETTUCE

Lactuca sativa

A green salad that includes a variety of heirloom lettuces can be one of the most flavorful and interesting parts of your meal. Old varieties of lettuce come in many shapes (oak leaf, "deer tongue") and colors (deep red, green with liberal spots of maroon), and the fresh taste far surpasses most grocery-store offerings.

Many heirloom varieties also come with stories: ancient Egyptians left drawings of huge romaine-style heads, and Thomas Jefferson was especially fond of a butterhead variety the size of a tennis ball. To establish lettuce as a plant every maritime gardener should cultivate, consider that it thrives in a cool, mild climate, with some varieties available for virtually every season.

Lettuce was first discovered growing wild in Asia Minor, and it was grown widely in ancient times. The earliest forms were leafy, with heading lettuce being developed by the sixteenth century. Columbus brought lettuce seeds to America on his second voyage,

Lettuce varieties

and some older varieties have been passed down from Canadian Mennonites. The variety of heirloom lettuces still available is more impressive than that of many other plants, making it truly a vegetable with staying power.

There are four types: loose-leaf or cutting lettuce, the standby in gourmet mesclun salad mixes; butterhead or Bibb lettuce, which forms loose heads with rounded leaves; head lettuce, like the standard grocery-store Iceberg; and romaine, a longer-leafed, upright, loose-heading type also known as cos because it was originally developed on the Greek island of Kos. It became "romaine" to French gardeners because it was famously grown in Rome, and that name caught on with American market gardeners. Butterhead is also known as Bibb, after the Kentucky judge Jack Bibb, who developed it in his greenhouse in 1865; Bibb lettuce salads have long been served with Kentucky Derby breakfasts.

CULTIVATION   Lettuce is best grown from seed directly sown, and with the ease of sprouting and the volume of seeds in a packet, there should be little reason to reach for a four-pack of starts in the nursery. It can be started in flats, thinned carefully, and transplanted precisely. The seeds need light to germinate, so just barely cover with a dusting of compost.

Lettuce does like air circulation, so thin to 8 inches apart in rows spaced a foot or more apart. Loose-leaf varieties are an exception: their seeds can be broadcast into a bed and allowed to grow thickly. The lettuce bed should have fertile, well-draining soil and should be oriented so that it doesn't receive the heat of the sun in high summer. Lettuce is a cool-season crop, but if you want to sow it in summer, planting between rows of taller vegetables can help.

Sow repeatedly in spring, every three weeks or so, and choose varieties that mature at different times for a continuous supply. For summer growing, choose a more robust type, such as romaine. Water regularly, but don't mulch around lettuce—that simply provides a hiding place for slugs and snails.

HARVEST AND STORAGE

The loose-leaf varieties offer "cut-and-come-again" convenience: you can shear a batch of leaves when they reach 4 to 6 inches in length, and the plant will send up more leaves. Some gardeners contend that subsequent cuttings are less flavorful. Harvest romaine, butterhead, and head lettuces by cutting off the whole head at the base. All three should be picked at the height of ripeness once they have reached their mature size, as overripe lettuces can become watery or bitter, which certainly happens after they begin to bolt.

Take full advantage of your ability to beat the grocery store by bringing lettuce straight from the garden, washing it, and using it immediately. If necessary, store it unwashed for two to three days, wrapped loosely in plastic, in the refrigerator's crisper.

SEED SAVING

Lettuce will bolt and form a seed head after maturing, especially in summer; but choose to save seed from the plant that bolts last, not first. That way you will preserve the most desirable trait. The length of the summer is crucial to getting fully mature seed. The seed is ready to harvest when it forms wispy, dandelion-like balls on plants that can get to 3 feet tall. When the seeds are nearly ripe, the seed head develops a feathery appearance, at which time you can cut the stalk and lay it to dry in a shady warm place, or enclose it in a paper bag. When the seed heads are fully dry, crush them to release the seed, and strain through a one-eighth-inch screen or winnow the chaff away from the seed in a light breeze. Be careful when winnowing, as the seed is nearly as light as the chaff.

TIP Grow your own mesclun! The word *mezclar* is Spanish for "to mix," hence our popular mesclun mélange of salad greens. To make your own mix, grow a variety of lettuces to be ready for harvest successively. But don't stop there: include other leafy, healthful greens from beets, spinach, chard, kale, endive, corn salad, and radicchio. Asian greens and mustards will add even more flavor, style, and zing.

VARIETIES

Black-Seeded Simpson
A classic of the loose-leaf lettuces, this variety has been in the U.S. since 1850 and is still widely grown. Its light-green, curled leaves are crisp and juicy. It is so easy to grow: it comes in early, is heat- and drought-resistant, and is rarely bitter.

Forellenschluss
The name of this old Austrian variety means "speckled like a trout," and it shows off with a burst of red and maroon freckles splashed upon a soft green field. It forms a medium-sized, loose romaine head of buttery leaves. In 1996, Seed Savers Exchange grew out its entire collection of 750 lettuces, and this one—which had been obtained from the European seed organization Arche Noah—emerged as a favorite.

Green Deer Tongue
The thick, spearhead-shaped leaves of this variety, which obviously reminded early growers of a deer's tongue, form a spiraling rosette of succulent, olive-green leaves growing to 8 inches long in

an upright, loose head. Introduced in 1740, it became a favorite of the Amish people, who developed their own varieties.

A baby romaine lettuce introduced to this country from England, Little Gem produces a cup of elongated oval leaves curving together into a small head. It is crisp and sweet, and in recent years has become popular under the name Sucrine (from the French word for "sugar") on trendy restaurant menus.

Little Gem

A variety that is quite responsive to the sun, this heirloom will color its lobed oaken curves with shades of red. It can handle more heat than some loose-leaf varieties, but will last well into the cooler fall weather as well. Seeds of Change named it a good choice for the maritime climate.

Red Oak Leaf

Dating from the 1840s and developed in France, this hardy romaine variety will withstand the weather and provide lovely deep red leaves for your winter salad. Leaves are buttery and mildly sweet.

Rouge d'Hiver

A close second in flashiness to Forellenschluss, this Mennonite heirloom that came to the U.S. from the Ontario, Canada, region also offers sprays and splotches of maroon across green leaves that pale to yellow along the rib. It is a small butterhead variety.

Speckled

Famously grown by Thomas Jefferson at a time when lettuce was pickled in brine or boiled, this is a great heading variety to grow in a small garden. Pale green leaves form loose heads that can grow larger than its name would imply, to 7 inches across. Texture of the gently folded leaves is silky, and the flavor is quite mild. This variety has also been marketed as Brown Dutch or Salamander (food historian William Woys Weaver notes that the latter is the older name), and there is a similar, white-seeded variety commonly called Boston Market. Jefferson wrote in his voluminous garden

Tennisball Black-Seeded

jottings that it required less attention than other varieties. It performs best in cool temperatures, and was often grown in winter cold frames to supply the early spring markets.

Tom Thumb   A small-headed, black-seeded variety similar to Tennisball (and a worthy substitute if you can't find the latter in seed catalogs), Tom Thumb produces very small heads, 5 inches or less, consisting of loosely formed, crinkled green leaves. It is an English heirloom that was introduced to Americans in the 1868 seed catalog of James J. Gregory of Marblehead, Massachusetts.

Onions

Allium cepa

Where would our meals be without the onion? It has long been an integral part of the human diet. One of the oldest cultivated plants, it has caused cooks to tear up for more than 3,500 years. It's not the easiest vegetable to grow, but once you understand its needs and find appropriate varieties, you'll be rewarded by providing yourself with this essential seasoning plant that produces in a relatively small space.

Originating in Asia and lands around the Mediterranean, the onion was grown extensively by the Egyptians. It was thought to have medicinal properties, and ancient Greek athletes would consume mass quantities of onions and onion juice before competitions to strengthen them. The onion was one of the staples in meat-and-potatoes England when America was colonized, and early settlers brought onions with them. It wasn't a new vegetable to Native Americans, however, who were already eating wild onion species.

The diversity of onion choices and flavors is impressive. Some, like the Northwest favorite Walla Walla, are said to be so sweet they can be eaten like an apple (but for me, I'll take an apple). While softball-like globe onions set the supermarket standard, home gardeners will find delightful choices in many shapes, from hockey pucks to bowling pins. *Allium cepa* also includes the multiplier onion, which forms clumps of individual small bulbs around a seed bulb, and the topsetting onion (also known as the tree, walking, or Egyptian onion), which forms small bulbs underground but also sends up a stalk that produces small bulbils at its peak.

Many seed companies offer onions, both as seeds and as starts. A quality supplier will generally ship starts at the right time for planting in your area. However, many heirloom varieties are not easily found as starts, so growing them from seed may be necessary.

Day length is key to growing onions. "Long-day" varieties are those planted in the northern areas, and so are right for Pacific Northwest maritime climates. There are also "short-day" varieties, planted south of latitude 36° (about the Kansas/Oklahoma border). The growth of an onion is spurred by its photoperiodic cycle, which

Cipollini Borrettana

uses the amount of daylight to tell the plant when to start bulbing. Long-day varieties need a photoperiod of fifteen to sixteen hours, while short-day varieties need eleven to twelve hours. Onion leaves relate to the rings of the bulb, so the more leaves present, the more rings will be seen. Once bulbing begins, top growth stops, so to get a large onion you must grow varieties that put on good top growth before the day length reaches twelve hours.

CULTIVATION Gardeners will have more assured success by planting bulbing and bunching onions from starts, rather than from seed, although some say onions from seed will become more flavorful. Multiplier and topsetting onions are started from bulbs harvested from the previous year's plant.

Start seed indoors very early in the spring, six to eight weeks before transplanting. Sow the seeds thickly, feed with a high-nitrogen liquid fertilizer, and try to get them to 6 inches or so before planting out. Harden off the seedlings, then trim the tops to 4 inches or so, and separate to 4 to 6 inches apart for bulbing onions, 2 inches apart for bunching onions. Trimmed tops will allow more energy to be spent on the roots, and the clippings can be used like chives in a salad.

Onion starts will generally be offered in bunches and will arrive as bare-root plants, so they must be planted promptly. Dig a trench, lay the seedlings in it at proper spacing, water well, and then fill in the trench, straightening the plants as you go. Plant topsetting onion bulbs at the same time as starts.

Onions like a rich soil with good drainage. They are heavy feeders with shallow roots. Amend the soil with a balanced organic fertilizer before planting, and then side-dress with a high-nitrogen fertilizer during leaf growth. Onions don't compete well with weeds, but cultivate the bed carefully so as to not damage shallow roots. Do not grow them too close together because they need air circulation to avoid molds and mildews in a maritime climate. A sea breeze is great.

Multiplier onions should be planted out in the fall, the same as garlic. Some longer-season varieties, such as Walla Walla Sweet, can be planted in the fall in mild climates and allowed to overwinter.

When tops of globe and multiplier onions begin to fall over and show signs of drying, withhold water so that you can harvest from dry soil. When half of the tops have fallen, push the rest over and leave them for a week. Then dig them up carefully, shake most of the soil off them, and lay them to dry on the soil, covering them as necessary so dew or rain won't remoisten them. If harvesting during extremely hot weather, cure them in partial shade or in the garage. After another week, trim the tops off about one inch above the bulb and remove the rest of the dried soil.

HARVEST AND STORAGE

The bulbils of topsetting onions can be harvested as they appear; they are great for pickling, or they can be replanted throughout the fall. The clumps can also be dug up, divided, and replanted.

Curing onions hardens the skin and allows longer storage. Store them in breathable mesh onion bags in a very cool location, and check regularly for sprouting or rotting ones. Storage length is dependent upon variety.

Onions are biennial, so they will send up their puffy, round seed heads in their second year. They are bee-pollinated and will readily cross, so the gardener must either separate varieties by a half-mile or leave only one variety to go to seed. Up to twenty seed plants might be needed to avoid weaker future stock. When the tops yellow and dry, shake the seed out or rub the head between your palms. Seed is hard, black, and irregularly shaped, and lasts only one year. Topsetting onions will produce topsetting seed on a stalk,

SEED SAVING

which will flop over, and often this seed will root when touching the ground. Multiplier onions (sometimes called potato onions) will produce bunches of onions around the main bulb.

TIP   Explore the many branches of the onion genus. Bunching onions, chives, garlic, leeks, and shallots are all part of the clan.

Bunching onions (*A. cepa* or *A. fistulosum*) don't form bulbs. They are planted thickly and then thinned by harvesting clumps of them—a good way to get green onions for salads and garnishes before the regular onion crop has come in. They are sometimes called pearl onions, or even categorized as scallions, but technically the latter term refers to bulbing onions harvested when immature.

Chives (*A. schoenoprasum*) are a perennial, from which you trim individual leaves for green onion flavors in salads, marinades, or other fresh uses. Dig up and divide the plant every three years. Their colorful pink flowers—multiple small stars on a compact head—can be used fresh as soon as they open to both brighten and spice up a salad. Garlic chives (*A. tuberosum*) offer fresh garlic flavor in a plant with the same properties as chives.

Garlic (*A. sativum*) and leeks (*A. ampeloprasum*) have wonderful heirloom varieties and are covered separately in this book.

Shallots (*A. ascalonicum*) are milder than onions and are highly valued in gourmet cooking. They form clumps with individual bulbs like bunching onions. They can be set out like garlic in the fall, or planted in the spring.

VARIETIES

Cipollini Borrettana   A flattened, button-shaped onion, this variety is a gem that produces marvelously in a maritime climate. It is an Italian heirloom that braids well and provides a striking addition to the kitchen at a fraction of its pricy market cost. Brown with a pale red blush, it grows 2 to 4 inches across and perhaps 1 inch thick. The flesh is mild and sweet. Harvested small, these onions are great skewered on kebabs, while larger ones are fantastic roasted, braised, or pickled (the last being their traditional use).

Danvers Yellow Globe

A medium-sized, long-day cooking onion that is very reliable in northern climates. It is thought to have originated in Danvers, Massachusetts, bred from the Common Yellow, and was introduced to France before 1850, according to the comprehensive garden book by the French writers Messrs. Vilmorin-Andrieux from that era. It produces a brown or coppery colored, slightly flattened globe, perhaps 3 inches in diameter. It has a medium pungency and is crisp and solid.

Egyptian Walking

Also known as tree or topsetting, this unique member of the genus provides an interesting onion that is useful year-round. The perennial plant puts up a sturdy flower stalk that holds a group of hazelnut-sized, purple-tinged bulbils which, when they grow and get heavy, cause the stalk to flop over. Some bulbils hit the ground and take root, which is how the plant "walks." You can use the new shoots as fresh onions in spring, but also harvest the bulbils for use (they're great for pickling) or replant them. Vegetable historian and author William Woys Weaver decries its identification as Egyptian, because he has found no solid connection to Egypt for its origin, but that is the name under which it is often sold.

Walla Walla Sweet

This mild, juicy bulb onion came to the Washington State town of Walla Walla in the 1880s in the hands of a French soldier who brought the seed from the island of Corsica. The area's Italian immigrant farmers began cultivating it, and perfected a variety so well loved and so identified with the area that it became the official Washington State vegetable in 2007. Can grow quite large in dryland conditions, but generally gets 3 to 4 inches across in maritime climates. Extremely high in water content, it will not store well, so use it shortly after its early summer harvest.

PEAS

Pisum sativum

Here is a simple recipe for sprouting the next generation of gardeners: Get your children to plant peas. Deceptively simple, yet effective. Peas seem to be the only vegetable many young children will eat, and once they've gotten a chance to try a sugar pea straight off the vine, or to plop a plump seed into a planting hole and watch it grow, they'll be hooked. Or, rather, ensnared by the vines and tendrils of the pea.

Peas, along with cherry tomatoes, are candy on a trellis, providing a burst of natural sugars to perk up your gardening tasks. But well before the harvest, the fascination of watching the pea vines sprout and climb so early in the gardening season will also capture the imagination, as the new shoots embody the exuberant attitude of spring.

But peas were not always embraced as nature's sugar snack. Originating in areas from western Asia to southern Europe, they were among the earliest domesticated crops. The pea was first a shelled vegetable that was cooked, its solid starch bulking up soups and stews. A Norse legend that resonates with my Scandinavian background was that pea soup was always eaten on Thursday, because peas were the favorite food of the ancient god Thor, and Thursday was Thor's day. Indeed, peas were not eaten fresh until the mid-seventeenth century, when the Dutch people introduced the *petits pois* type to France. They became all the rage in the French aristocracy, and once they were embraced by the royal court their popularity was assured.

Peas were brought to the U.S. by colonists, and were said to be Thomas Jefferson's favorite vegetable. His extensive garden book lists over fifty varieties, and he even held a contest with his neighbors to see who could put the first spring peas on the table. The winner would provide a dinner, which included a pea dish, for the other contestants. Our third president was an accomplished gardener, but there is no record of his ever winning the contest, although he often provided the party and the meal. Perhaps a pea contest would be an appropriate new summer event to honor the most horticultural of our leaders.

Three kinds of peas are commonly grown: shelling, sugar, and snap.

Shelling peas, as the name implies, are broken open and only the seed (called the "berry") is eaten. Usually, these are quite plump and large, and tend to be less sweet and more starchy. Some varieties have smooth berries, others wrinkle as they dry. They can be eaten fresh, but many shelling peas come to the table cooked, or are dried and then reconstituted for use.

Snow peas, also known as sugar peas, are eaten in an immature form while the berry is still quite small, and the entire pod is picked and eaten. The slightly

Tall Telephone

swelling seeds can be seen through the thin walls of the flattened pods. These peas can be eaten raw, or tossed into a stir-fry in the last minute of cooking. The tendrils of some varieties are a delicacy, too, eaten steamed or stir-fried.

Snap peas also have berries that are fully formed, or nearly so. These "edible-podded" varieties are usually eaten like snap beans, lightly cooked, although some varieties can be eaten raw. They are of modern origin, so there are no heirloom snap peas.

In the quest for a sweeter pea, hybrids have become the norm, and that's what mostly fills the seed racks and catalog pages. But seeds are easy to save, so heirloom gardeners can undertake a quest to find their favorite old pea and perpetuate it in their garden. In the ultimate show of respect for the old-timers, share seed with friends!

CULTIVATION   As I've suggested, planting peas is the perfect first gardening task for small hands. Help them in a few areas: choosing the location, lightly amending the soil, warding off common diseases, and creating a trellis for the peas to climb.

Plant peas in a spot that gets sun early in the season, where a trellis thick with vines won't shade other midspring plants that need the sun. It should also be very accessibly sited because regular, nearly daily, pickings are necessary for productivity. Often a long row on a sturdy trellis is best. For the vining varieties, a trellis or something to help them climb a fence is a necessity, and even bush varieties will benefit from support, although some may be left to grow as a mound.

Peas can be planted as soon as the ground can be worked. They do not tolerate heavy soil that doesn't drain well. Digging in organic matter and a bit of balanced fertilizer will get them off to a good start. Side-dress with a complete fertilizer after the tendrils begin to climb.

When planting, create a shallow furrow and cover the seeds with 1 to 2 inches of soil. Yields may be increased by pre-coating the seeds with a legume inoculant, which boosts the presence of beneficial bacteria in the soil so the plants can attach more nitrogen to their root systems. Peas should be direct-sown if possible, as they do not take well to transplanting. Plants may be close, as little as 1 to 2 inches apart. For bush peas, space rows 18 to 24 inches apart; for climbers, two trellises can be placed 6 inches apart, with seeds planted on the outside edge of each. Practice succession planting to extend the pea harvest, which can reach into midsummer.

HARVEST AND STORAGE

Begin to pick when the peas reach their stated size per variety; regular picking will encourage more flowering and dramatically increase productivity. Here again is a good opportunity for young hands to get active. Children love discovering peas on the vines, and if they are taught the two-handed picking method (grasp the vine near the pea with one hand, gently twist the pea from the vine with the other), they will be good garden helpers. They have the advantage of seeing the vines at eye level or looking up into the plant, although adults may be called upon to get the high-hanging pods.

Sugar and snap peas are best when eaten fresh from the garden but can be stored unwashed in the refrigerator crisper for a couple of days if necessary. Many varieties also take well to blanching and freezing for later use. Shelling peas should be shelled immediately upon picking and then cooked, frozen, or allowed to dry, depending upon the use. Shelling peas left on the vine past ripeness will get starchy and tough, so continual monitoring at harvest time is essential.

SEED SAVING

Peas are self-pollinating, so saving seed is an easy proposition. However, bees love to visit the flowers, so cross-pollinating can occur. To minimize this problem for seed saving, plant varieties at least 25 feet apart, or grow another tall plant as a shield between varieties. Pick peas as their pods dry, then shell and air-dry fully. To test for maturity, bite down on a pea; if your teeth don't leave a mark, it's dry. To avoid fungal growth, store the seeds in a breathable material like paper or burlap, not in plastic.

TIP   Pea tendrils have become popular as an early spring side dish in recent years, and you can harvest these for eating without sacrificing too much of your crop. Sow the peas thickly, perhaps 1 inch apart, and allow a significant tangle of plants. Cut tendrils when they reach 12 to 18 inches and the curly ends are starting to grab at the trellis. Chop them, stir-fry with spring garlic until just wilted, and enjoy the delicate pea flavor.

VARIETIES

Alaska   Named not for the state but for a fast steamship, Alaska was introduced in 1880 and is a quick-growing, early producer of shelling peas. Not as sweet as some varieties, but great for soup. Plants are 2 to 3 feet tall, and 3-inch pods offer five or six small green peas.

Blue-Podded   This is a classic soup pea. Sometimes the pods are purple rather
` Capajuner   than blue, but either way this is a striking variety to grow as an ornamental vine. The large vines produce a heavy crop of 4- to 6-inch blue, rounded pods that stand out from soft green foliage. The pods can be eaten like snow peas when very young, or the mature peas can be shelled and dried.

Dwarf Grey Sugar   A sugar pea on a plant that grows to 30 inches, this has been the standard pea since Revolutionary times. It is one of the earliest-producing peas, offering sweet, 2- to 3-inch pods in less than two months.

Also called Homesteader, this variety of shelling pea dates to 1908. **Lincoln**
It is a dwarf vining pea that grows to 30 inches and produces 3- to
4-inch pods chock full of small, wrinkled peas. Great for small
gardens, and a good producer in the North.

Also called Alderman, this is another wrinkled-seeded shelling vari- **Tall Telephone**
ety that produces on vines 6 feet or more tall. It has been grown since
the 1700s. The pods are huge, producing six to eight flavorful, large
peas in prolific quantities. Matures later than some other varieties.

PEPPERS

Heat in the garden doesn't come only from the sun; it also comes *Capsicum annuum*
from within the spicy, waxy fruits of the pepper. When I see the
pendulous hot peppers turning red on my plants in late summer,
I smile in amazement at the fire contained in them. That warm
feeling returns, sometimes with a gasp, as I chop the colorful fruits
into my sauté pan. Long ago, during a celebratory Mexican cooking session, I happily chopped onions and peppers, and forgot that
their prep needs do not mix. The pungent onions caused my eyes
to tear up, and I reached with my pepper-chopping fingers to wipe
away the tears. You can imagine the rest: I spent the next hour red-
faced and beside myself with the burning sensation. It's something
you (hopefully) only do once, and people who are very sensitive
to the hot capsicum chemicals released in chopping would do well
to wear gloves and designate a separate knife and cutting board for
the task. But I lived to tell this cautionary tale, and I also recall the
meal being memorable for being topped with a freshly made salsa
that was ¡muy picante!

Peppers originated in Mexico, Central America, and South America at least 7,000 years ago, and an astonishing array of them still exists, particularly in Mexico and the southwestern U.S. Europeans were first made aware of peppers by Christopher Columbus, who discovered them on his first sailing to the New World, when he landed in the West Indies. Trying to describe the flavor and its use as a spice, he unfortunately called it "pepper," even though black pepper from the Far East was well known by that name and, in fact, was the most valued spice of the time. These new peppers traveled widely from Spain into Africa and the East before being brought by immigrants and slaves into colonized America. Other heirloom strains were adopted by settlers from the fields of Southwestern native peoples.

Contrary to the concerns of many maritime gardeners, peppers will generally produce in a cooler, northern climate, if perhaps not as vigorously as in a hot area. The plants may be smaller and their production lower, but even a few moderately hot peppers can spice up your cooking, so they are well worth including in the home garden.

CULTIVATION   Grow peppers as you would other members of the family Solanaceae (tomato, potato, and eggplant): in full sun, in well-draining soil amended with compost and a balanced fertilizer. Plant them 12 to 18 inches apart. Keep the plants well watered

Jimmy Nardello
Italian Sweet

through the season, and fertilize again when they begin to flower. Avoid a heavy dose of nitrogen, which would encourage more leaf growth at the expense of flower production.

In cooler climates, peppers benefit from being started indoors and transplanted out only after the weather is consistently warm. Territorial Seed Company advises planting them out two weeks after tomatoes go in the ground. Additional season-extending methods such as growing them under a cloche or in a Wall O' Water will aid early flowering and full maturity in some varieties.

Peppers are self-pollinating, but insects also love visiting the flowers, so cross-pollination can occur, and it usually results in mild peppers becoming hotter. To ensure that seed of each pepper is true to type, isolate plants by variety.

HARVEST AND STORAGE

Most peppers can be harvested and used fresh, although some hot varieties are excellent when dried and chopped into flakes or ground into powder. Regular picking as the fruits achieve size and color for their type will keep the plant setting flowers until late summer, although later fruits may not achieve full size.

Hot peppers that ultimately turn red can be picked and used at their green or intermediate stages—a good strategy to test for spiciness and enjoy the very hottest ones as they're ripening. Sweet peppers, however, may taste green or bitter if picked too early.

Once harvested, peppers will keep in the refrigerator crisper for two weeks or more or can continue to ripen and dry on the counter. Encourage proper drying by hanging an entire pepper plant upside down in a cool, dry place with good circulation.

SEED SAVING

Pepper seeds are quite easy to save, by either the wet or the dry method. For the wet method, scoop out the ribs with seed attached and immerse in a jar with water, then gently scrape the seeds from the rib. Discard the ribs and let the seeds sit in the water bath for two or three days, stirring and rinsing occasionally with clean water. When no more froth appears on the surface of the water, drain the seeds and spread them on a paper plate to dry fully. This wet-harvesting method ensures that the seeds will be free of any disease or fungus. Saving by the dry method of just scooping the seeds from the fruit and spreading them on a paper plate also works, but disease can be carried with the seed.

TIP   Do you have aphids, spider mites, whiteflies, leaf hoppers, or other chewing/sucking pests on your vegetables? A blast of *Capsicum annuum* might shoo them away. There are a number of commercial sprays made from hot peppers that claim to provide safe, natural pest control. You can also make your own liquid spray. Don a pair of gloves, chop up a bunch of hot peppers, and then let them soak in water for a couple of days. Strain the pepper chunks out, mix the water with a bit of biodegradable soap to help the mixture stick, then spray it on leafy greens, legumes, tomatoes, and other crops where you see damage. But don't bother spraying it on peppers; they can defend themselves.

VARIETIES

Bull Nose   A large bell pepper with wonderfully crunchy, thick flesh, Bull Nose has a distinctively blocky shape with a multilobed blunt tip that gives it its name. This mild pepper stays green to its full size of 4 by 3 inches, but becomes sweeter if left on its 2-foot-high plant to turn red. Also known as Bell or Large Sweet Spanish, it was grown in Thomas Jefferson's garden and became the most popular variety of the 1800s. Historians believe that what we grow today is not exactly the Bull Nose of Jefferson's day but more likely a strain developed later in the 1800s. It is an early pepper that can come to maturity in eighty days. It was widely renowned as a pickled pepper, but is great in salads or cooked.

Also known as Bull's Horn (in translation), this Italian heirloom is a sweet pepper that tapers to a point like a bull's horn. Yellow or red fruit gets 4 inches long, growing on vigorous plants. It has a mild flavor that is excellent on the grill or in the frying pan. It was introduced into the U.S. before 1920.

Corno di Toro

A beautiful and tasty combination of plant and fruit. Its plants can reach 3 feet and produce a number of purple flowers on dark stems, with leaves also veined in purple. The 4-inch fruit tapers to a blunt end and ranges from dusky red to deep purple verging on black. It has a mild heat and can be enjoyed raw or cooked. A very short-season pepper, good for more northern climates.

Czech Black

We think of paprika peppers as being from Hungary, and indeed they were bred there and are proudly grown as one of that country's premier spice plants. However, like most types, paprika peppers originated in Mexico and Central America. Columbus took them to Europe, and they made their way to Hungary through trading with southern Europeans. Feher Ozon is a short-season star, used for drying and grinding but also for fresh eating. The productive plant delivers 3- to 4-inch sweet fruits with smooth, orange-to-red skins about seventy days after transplanting.

Feher Ozon Paprika

An African-American heirloom grown by people enslaved to work on Southern plantations, this is a hot crunchy pepper with a bold flavor. Both the plants and the fruit are variegated: the leaves are minty green with white or cream ribbing, while the fruits are white with green stripes when young, maturing to red via an intermediate stage when they are orange with brown stripes. Commonly grown in the areas around Chesapeake Bay, this pepper is not

Fish

surprisingly a traditional spice in shellfish dishes. It is listed in Slow Food USA's Ark of Taste as a food with a significant history.

Hungarian Hot Wax Also known as Hungarian Yellow or Hot Banana, this long, banana-shaped pepper turns from green to yellow, but keeps going to red. It carries a medium-hot rating, and often is used pickled or canned. It has smooth flesh in tapered, 6-inch fruits that sometimes grow pointing upwards or at odd angles.

Jimmy Nardello Italian Sweet Called the ultimate frying pepper, this slender, knobby pepper has a fruity taste when raw that becomes creamy when fried. Originally from the southern Italy region of Basilicata, it was brought to this country by Italian immigrant Jimmy Nardello, who moved to Connecticut in 1887. The curling, tapered fruits can get up to 10 inches long, on 2-foot-tall plants. It is also listed in Slow Food USA's Ark of Taste heritage program.

POTATOES

Solanum tuberosum

When I was growing up on a farm in North Dakota, potatoes were a major staple in my family's garden. We grew enough that sometimes it seemed that was all our large family ate. They survived in the cellar long after delicate fruits of the garden like tomatoes were consumed or canned. Although the popularity of low-carb diets has reduced America's potato consumption, the venerable root crop has come back into vogue, largely because a new generation of small, organic farmers has exposed the public to a great array of choices. The home gardener, too, has an opportunity to grow more varieties than ever, from meal-sized white bakers to delicate fingerlings that are bite-sized and brightly colored. Although many are recent hybrids, some fantastic heirloom potatoes are available, and some of them grow quite well in the maritime climate.

The consummate heirloom potato for the maritime Northwest is the Ozette. It carries the cachet of coming straight from the center of origin for potatoes: the Andes in South America. Potatoes were a staple in the diet of the Inca people, and were depicted on ancient Peruvian pottery. The Ozette, a knobby yellowish variety, was brought by Spanish explorers from South America to the Northwest coast, where they shared it with the Makah Indian people living in a community called Ozette. There it was grown for many years, but was very nearly lost. In recent years, renewed interest and a listing in Slow Food USA's Ark of Taste has put it on the rebound, and today it sometimes can be found at farmers markets and in seed catalogs.

On the East Coast, potatoes were brought by colonists from Ireland who settled in Londonderry, New Hampshire, in 1719. Many new varieties were developed in the U.S. and exported to Europe, and today the most famous varieties, such as the Russet Burbank, were developed here.

CULTIVATION

Potatoes need loose, well-draining soil, so dig compost in liberally if soil is at all heavy. They need phosphorus, so bonemeal is a good addition. They prefer a pH level toward the acidic side, so gypsum can be added if necessary. Plant midspring, when the ground has warmed somewhat; if it is too cold, the potato pieces will rot before they can sprout.

Potatoes are generally planted by cutting a whole seed potato into pieces that contain two or three eyes each. Small potatoes can be planted whole. Cut the potatoes just before planting, and don't allow the pieces to dry out: the young roots will feed off the moisture and nutrients in the potato piece as they take hold. You can trigger seed potatoes into sprouting by exposing them to moderate warmth and light for a week or so before planting.

You can plant seed pieces 4 to 6 inches deep in a hole and cover them completely, but a method of getting more potatoes is to plant more deeply in a trench that you will fill in as the potato vines grow. Dig trenches 12 to 14 inches deep and 3 feet apart, and drop in seed pieces at least a foot apart. Cover the seeds with 4 to 6 inches of soil. When the vines are about 6 inches tall, backfill the trench to one-third the height of the vines. Continue to do this whenever vines have put on another 6 inches of growth, until the soil reaches ground level, and then once more, this time hilling up the soil around the growing plants with a hoe, which has the side benefit of weeding the bed at the same time. This practice results in more roots being produced along the stems, and tubers growing close to those stems, which makes for easier harvest.

Keep the potato bed well weeded and moderately watered; overwatering results in watery potatoes with less flavor.

Watch for potato beetles hiding among the leaf stems and setting their yellow egg clusters on the undersides of the leaves. Destroy

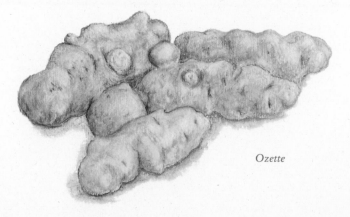

Ozette

the beetles and eggs immediately and mercilessly. To avoid common potato diseases like late blight and verticillium wilt, remove any diseased plants immediately, and rotate your plantings; don't grow potatoes or other nightshade-family plants (tomatoes, peppers, and eggplants) in the bed again for three years.

Watch for blossoms at about two months after planting, and then begin to reach into the soil around the base of the plant to check for new potatoes. Some can be harvested as the plant grows, and they are tender and delicious. No need to let these cure—use them right away.

HARVEST AND STORAGE

Dig potatoes after vines have wilted and are dry to the ground level. They generally only wilt after frost, so if you're in a region with no frost, dig one plant to test for size. If you want to harvest but plants are still growing, break or chop the stems to stop growth and then wait for them to die back. Leave the tubers in the ground for two weeks after dieback to toughen the skins and ready them for storage.

When digging, use a garden fork, not a shovel. Start loosening the soil well away from the center of the plant and work inward. Your goal is to not skewer or bruise any potatoes.

Air-dry potatoes in the garden after harvest if possible, and then store them in a cool dark place, checking regularly to see if they're rotting or sprouting. Any nicked or scabby potatoes should be used first. Store in burlap sacks or something else breathable. Special note: Discard potatoes with green skin immediately, even if it's just a spot of green, because these are poisonous and must not be eaten.

Some catalogs carry both seed potatoes and potato seed, which are actually two different things. Seed potatoes are those potatoes held out of a mature crop to be used for seed. But potatoes also produce

SEED SAVING

flowers, and some of those flowers go to seed or, to be more precise, to berries. These are sometimes called "true seed." The berries are generally sprouted indoors like tomatoes, and then planted out and grown with regular potato culture.

TIP   Cage 'em. If you're short on garden real estate, grow your potatoes in a cage for a high yield in a compact space. Arrange a bottomless wire cage, or a barrel or other container, over a plot of garden soil. The container should be at least 18 inches in diameter and 3 to 4 feet high. It must be able to hold soil and compost. Set a potato seed or a piece containing at least one eye on the ground in the center of the cage, and cover with 4 to 6 inches of a soil/compost mixture. Keep the soil moist until vines appear. As the vines grow, keep adding layers of soil, making sure you don't cover more than a quarter or a third of the exposed vine. This temporary raised bed will dry out fast, so keep an eye on the moisture content. When the vines start to flower, stop adding soil. Harvest in the same way as plants grown in the ground. This is a great technique for small or fingerling potatoes.

VARIETIES

Bintje   Also called Yellow Finnish, this late-season variety came to the U.S. from the Netherlands in 1911 and today is one of the most widely grown of its type. The skin tends toward brown, but the flesh is a buttery yellow. Its midsized, oblong tubers are good for all uses.

Ozette   Sometimes called Anna Cheeka's Ozette, this large, late-season fingerling was brought to the Makah Indians on Washington State's Olympic Peninsula by Spanish explorers in the 1700s. It's knobby and gnarly, but the long, slender potato has mild, creamy yellow flesh.

A favorite for all-around cooking and keeping, this long-maturing fingerling is dry and low in starch. Nearly purple skin covers yellow flesh.

Rose Finn Apple

Introduced in 1876 by the venerable plant breeder Luther Burbank, this is the potato instantly identified with Idaho, and it grows well in the maritime climate if given consistent water. Its large, oval tubers have dusky tan skin that is heavily "russeted," or marbled with a dark brown tinge and rough texture. Flesh is white, fine-grained, perfect for baking. A midseason variety that keeps well.

Russet Burbank

A golden fingerling that is renowned for its flavor, with a waxy texture that's great in potato salads. Came to the U.S. through British Columbia, where it was grown by early settlers. It is a late-season variety, taking over ninety days to mature.

Russian Banana

PUMPKINS

Growing pumpkins can be one of the most exciting gardening adventures for a child, especially if the family celebrates Halloween by carving them up into jack-o-lanterns. Watching the fruit swell, rise above the vine's leaves, and turn from green to orange is a treat of discovery. A field of pumpkins among the wilted vines is a quintessential image of autumn. The Thanksgiving holiday, too, proves much richer in tradition due to the pumpkin. A sweet and creamy deep-orange pie seems to be the perfect finale to a turkey dinner. So try an heirloom pumpkin with both uses in mind, knowing that you're preserving tradition in the garden as well as on the porch and the table.

Cucurbita pepo,
C. maxima

CULTIVATION

The main concern when you're growing pumpkins is space. A field or an untended area of the garden is ideal. In the maritime climate, an additional consideration is having enough heat to get the vines going so they'll set fruit that will ripen in a shorter summer.

Get a jump-start on garden heat by starting the seeds indoors in late spring, perhaps three weeks before the last frost date. Keep soil barely damp when sprouting so that the seeds don't rot. Don't start them too early; the soil must be in the 60-degree range with predictable warm weather before the seedlings can be planted out. If left indoors too long, they will become leggy and rootbound and won't set their roots properly in the soil when planted, so transplant them just as they're getting a second set of true leaves. Pumpkins have a delicate root system, so start them in a peat pot or recycled-newspaper pot that can be set into the soil with the plant and decompose as the vine grows.

Prepare the ground as you would for other squashes. Pumpkins

Cinderella

are medium-feeders and require regular water, so add a balanced fertilizer and plenty of compost. Vines often do well in hills. Create a mound of soil with enough flat space on top for three small plants set 1 foot apart. Keep the hill weeded as they grow, taking care not to disturb the root systems. Covering the hill with a floating row cover or cloche can increase the heat and give the young plants a boost until summer takes hold. Pull the cover away as flowers appear—the plants need bees and other flying insects for pollination.

HARVEST AND STORAGE

Pumpkins are best if cured partially in the field, so unless you antic-ipate very wet weather, leave them until their vines have started to die back. Cut off each pumpkin, leaving an inch or two of stem attached, and move it to a cool, dry location for further curing, which often will increase the sugar content. Never pick up the fruit by the stem (it is not a handle) because rot will begin at the point of a broken stem. Pumpkins should be fully cured after two to three weeks, although some varieties can store fine for months. Regularly monitor the fruit in storage for soft spots or color change, and use or process immediately if you see any deterioration.

SEED SAVING

Tag the best fruit specimen and harvest it normally. Curing it after harvest will increase seed viability. Scoop out the seeds, wash them in a colander and remove pulp, and then allow them to dry for two to three weeks on paper or a screen. Store in an airtight jar in a cool, dark place.

TIP

The older neighbor kids at our annual pumpkin-carving party have a great time making unique and quite scary faces using a cordless electric drill along with the more traditional carving tools. (Close adult supervision is definitely required.)

VARIETIES

Cinderella   Perhaps more commonly known by its French name Rouge Vif d'Etampes (sometimes listed as Red Etampes), this elegant pumpkin from the *C. maxima* species produces large, flattened fruits with deep creases running from stem to stern. It has a bright red hue that virtually glows. It was very popular in France through the 1800s, and W. Atlee Burpee brought it to this country in 1883. It can get up to 15 inches across and weigh more than 20 pounds. The dusky yellow flesh has a mild flavor and a texture less desirable than some, but is not stringy and can be baked or put into soups. One plant can produce up to six fruits on a vigorous, 15-foot vine, but it will take a long season, up to 130 days. The shell can be carved for Halloween, but you'll probably want to imprint a sweet face on it so you won't shatter the dreams of princesses who come to your door trick-or-treating; the pumpkin does indeed resemble Cinderella's coach.

Connecticut Field   These large globes are the standard for carving a jack-o'-lantern. The exterior of this *C. pepo* variety, also known as Big Tom or Yankee Cow, has numerous shallow ribs on dusky orange skin. The yellow-orange flesh is stringy and is generally not eaten. It is thought to be one of the oldest pumpkins grown in the U.S. and was very likely grown by the Indians before the colonists arrived. Fruits can get up to 20 pounds on vigorous vines.

Small Sugar   The premier pie pumpkin (in fact, it's also known as New England Pie), this *C. pepo* variety has smooth, creamy flesh that is bright orange and quite sweet. It has been grown in this country at least since the Civil War. You'll get four to six fruits from a plant that spreads vines to 10 feet or more. Each pumpkin, nearly round with light ribbing, will weigh in at 5 to 8 pounds, making it ideal for fresh use, although it also does well when canned or frozen.

RADICCHIO

Chicorium intybus

The striking red heads of radicchio, or red chicory, prove a unique, colorful addition to both the garden and the plate. It is one of two heading members of the *Chicorium* genus, which includes its leafy cousin, endive (given its own alphabetical listing above), and the root vegetable sometimes used in coffee, most famously in the French Market–brew style coffee of New Orleans. Of them all, radicchio is the most bitter and certainly the most striking in appearance.

Like lettuce, radicchio grows with little trouble, and it's another great crop for the cool maritime climate. A modest amount can spice up a salad like no other ingredient. Chicory was first brought to the U.S. from Europe in its root form, and in the eighteenth century the leaf and heading varieties began to be grown. Radicchio

Rossa de Treviso

has never been wildly popular in American gardens, but it has gained new attention in recent years when it was included in the gourmet salads in restaurants, and now is part of the mesclun mixes sold in markets.

CULTIVATION Start seeds indoors in midspring to transplant out; germination will be more successful than if they're direct-sown. For a winter crop, sow in midsummer and cut the first set of leaves to trigger the formation of a head. Soil should be well mulched and kept consistently watered while plants are young. Thin to at least a foot apart to allow space for ultimate sizing, and keep weeded. Radicchio is best eaten in winter, as it becomes less bitter and more sweet in cold weather. It also can be blanched to make it milder by covering it with an upturned pot for a week before harvest, but be watchful for slugs and snails that this method may attract.

HARVEST AND STORAGE Cut when leaves or heads have reached the predicted size per variety. With the loose-headed varieties, cut individual leaves for salads as needed. With heading varieties, cut off the entire head a half-inch above the soil, and discard the outer layer of leaves. The sturdy individual-leaf variety will hold up to a few days of storage, but the heading variety can last unwashed in the refrigerator for two weeks.

SEED SAVING Chicories are biennial, so plants must be saved in the ground or in pots for a second summer. Replant and let flower, then cut back water as the seeds develop. Seeds will be firm and dry in their hard pods when ripe.

TIP You can force the romaine-style looser-leaf radicchio to form a tighter head by wrapping the leaves loosely together with twine.

VARIETIES

Named for the Italian town where it originated, this striking (and
currently trendy) variety has speckles of pink and wine red on
pale yellow leaves. Outer leaves fold loosely around a lettucelike
head in the manner of a rose, giving it the nickname "the edible
flower." Its mild flavor, with an agreeable, slightly bitter edge, can
be enjoyed raw in a salad.

Castelfranco

This is a loose-heading variety that comes from the Treviso area
of Italy. Instead of a tight, round ball of leaves, it's a grouping of
elongated, spoon-shaped leaves. Leaves are green in summer but
turn red by maturity in midautumn. Slightly bitter taste, although
milder than some.

Rossa di Treviso

RADISH

Raphanus sativus

The quick-growing radish is a peppery staple of the spring vegetable garden, but there are winter-keeping ones that will elevate your
radish senses to new heights. And, though the vegetable has taken
a minor place at the modern gardener's table, its history shows a
position of importance. Originally from China, over the centuries
radishes have been used medicinally (they are high in vitamin C),
grown as peasant food, prized by nobility, and tossed into dishes
as a spice. They are truly a root crop that has seen the highs and
lows of popularity. Most recently, the spring radish's role has been
as a crunchy bit of peppery redness in a sea of salad greens or rel-
ish tray displays. In Asian cooking, its relative daikon has earned a
place in stir-fries and pickling.

Spring radishes are cheery vegetables, popping up earlier than

French Breakfast

most other direct-sown seeds, pushing their shoulders out of the ground as they grow, and providing a harvest while most other root crops are still being thinned to their ultimate spacing. They mature on about the same schedule as lettuce, convenient for tossing into the spring salad bowl. The exposed top of the round or oblong varieties anchors a spray of leaves, sprouting in soft green tones, that are slightly prickly to the touch. Although they aren't often eaten today, the leaves are in fact edible, carrying a milder flavor of the peppery root.

Best known are the red globe varieties that are spring supermarket staples, and that group includes the elegant French Breakfast, an elongated variety with red roots tapering gently to white tips. You can range farther afield with yellow- or white-skinned varieties. That early adopter Thomas Jefferson grew eight kinds of radishes, from black to salmon to scarlet to white.

Winter-storage radishes, such as the Asian daikon or the large black Spanish, take radish-growing to new depths and widths as well as to another season. Daikon varieties can easily grow 1 to 2 feet in length, and the large black roots of the Spanish varieties seem to be more akin to turnips or beets.

CULTIVATION   Radishes will thrive in a loose, sandy soil, especially when thinned to provide ample spacing, 1 to 2 inches apart for most varieties. Some spring varieties mature in as little as three weeks. Plant seeds of the small spring radish as early as the soil can be worked, but follow different timing for daikon or the longer-season black varieties. Succession planting will greatly extend the time for radishes on the table, so plant a short row each week up until early summer. Most varieties will quickly bolt or turn woody if planted in the warmest summer weather. Plantings can take place again from late summer to midautumn, or in a cold frame in a maritime garden. Because they have shallow roots, regular water is important; uneven growth can cause misshapen, woody, or hollow roots.

In the case of daikon varieties, planting time is very important. They too are cooler-weather crops, and some can overwinter. Plant varieties that show maturity dates of forty-five to sixty days in late spring; for varieties that indicate maturity of over sixty days, plant in fall and overwinter. Black Spanish varieties are planted in midsummer for fall harvest; they develop a thick skin that makes their heavy globes store well.

The word *daikon* is Japanese for "long root," and the spicy Asian varieties live up to the name. They can reach 2 feet or more, with roots 2 to 4 inches in diameter. The radish root pushes itself partially from the ground as it grows, and the tops can get large and bushy. The larger varieties can take sixty to eighty days to mature.

HARVEST AND STORAGE

Harvest spring radishes when they're just turning ripe. Waiting too long will result in tough roots that split or become fibrous, and they often develop a stronger, hotter taste as well. Close to the maturity date, begin to pull and test one radish a day. When ripe, pull them all for refrigerator storage, which is better than losing some by trying to keep them in the soil, as is the common practice with other root vegetables. They will keep, unwashed, for a week or so in a plastic bag in the crisper.

To harvest, dig around the plant carefully to avoid breaking the root. For longer storage, keep roots in damp sand in a cool place such as a basement.

SEED SAVING

Radishes send up a tall flower that produces seed pods. Since the plants are self-incompatible (that is, they can't use their own pollen to make seed), you need multiple plants flowering so that insects can distribute pollen among them. Varieties will freely cross, so for seed saving they must be isolated or only one variety must be left to flower at a time. The seed pods, which turn from green to brown, will dry on the stalk, but need a month or so in a paper bag to dry and mature.

TIP   A frequent suggestion is to interplant spring radishes with long-season crops, and the best pairing I've heard is with onions. A row of small radishes growing between the onion rows can be popped out of the soil before the onions start bulbing, and the onions' pungent odor will help fend off insects that would be destructive to the radish.

VARIETIES

French Breakfast   Named in the days when radishes were routinely eaten for break-fast, this elegant variety tastes as good as it looks. Elongated, blunt-tipped roots shaped like corks are richly red on the top three-quarters, changing to white at the end. They grow to 2 inches, with a third of the root above ground.

Helios   As can be inferred from the name (which comes from the Greek word for "sun"), this olive-shaped spring radish has a pale yellow exterior and white flesh.

Iwai Daikon   Smaller than many daikons, Iwai is a traditional variety served in special celebrations in Japan. It attains perhaps 1 inch in diameter and half the length of some varieties. Made into pickles or used in a soup, it will be found on many tables for New Year's dinner. Kitazawa Seed Company notes that it has been designated a tra-ditional vegetable of Nara, the city that served as the first capital of Japan.

Many American gardeners will find the black radish an oddity, it being so far from the supermarket ideal of a small red globe. This carrotlike tapered form, introduced in the U.S. before 1828, can get to 10 inches long and 3 inches thick in good soil, and has a rough, earthy appearance. Its tough black skin hides snowy white flesh that is as crisp and pungent as that of the more familiar variety. Even its tops are unusual and showy, with stems tending toward purple. These late-season, hardy radishes take well to storage. The traditional keeping method is to immerse them in layers of damp sand in a root cellar. A round version of this radish reaches 4 to 6 inches in diameter.

Long Black Spanish

SPINACH

Spinacia oleracea

This leafy green is truly a crop for the maritime climate, as it thrives in cool conditions and is a reliable producer when other greens are just struggling along. Some varieties can be planted in fall to overwinter, and some have proven to be very hardy, even in colder areas.

Called "spinage" when it was first grown in colonial America, spinach had been a part of European diets for many centuries. Historians have traced its path from Persia to the Far East, and then to Spain via the Moorish people of North Africa. In the sixteenth century, it became a favorite dish of Catherine de' Medici, an Italian aristocrat born in Florence who became queen of France. She would have dishes prepared on a bed of spinach, in a style that became known as "Florentine." Spinach was being sold in American seed catalogs by 1806.

Spinach is extremely nutritious, so minimal preparation is indicated. However, along with its vitamins and minerals, it contains oxalic acid, which can be hard on the digestive system and can block your body's absorption of calcium and iron. It also can impart a slightly sharp or bitter taste to the greens. Whether the amount of oxalic acid in raw spinach is harmful is debated, but the problem is solved when spinach is lightly cooked.

CULTIVATION   Prepare the spinach bed well with abundant fertilizer and compost. Plant seeds as early in the spring as possible, to provide the longest season before summer heat. Sow in succession every two weeks to extend the harvest. Be sure to give the plants plenty of room; they underperform when crowded. Thin to 3 inches apart in rows 12 inches apart. Fertilize partway through growing season.

Spinach does best when direct-sown into the beds, but it can be started in flats in a cool location. It needs consistent watering, especially before seed emergence. If later plantings are exposed to consistently warmer temperatures, the plants will be more likely to bolt, so shade from the sun if necessary.

When planting in fall for overwintering, pay special attention to preparing the bed with plenty of organic matter and fertilizer. Test for pH levels, and amend soil as necessary to provide a neutral pH (measuring 6.5 to 7.5). Plant after the heat of summer has passed, from late August through September in most maritime climates.

HARVEST AND
STORAGE   Pick individual leaves, or if a cutting bed of spinach is desired, the plant can be cut more severely and allowed to regrow. As the winter crop grows, harvest only lightly, taking the larger outer leaves from the plant.

Heavily crinkled varieties may need an extra washing to ensure that all the sandy grit is washed off the leaves, and all spinach will benefit from being plunged into ice water briefly before use or

*Long Standing
Bloomsdale*

storage. As with all greens, spinach should be used promptly, but it can last three or four days when washed and stored in a salad spinner or plastic bag in the refrigerator crisper.

Spinach plants are either male or female, so in order to produce viable seed, multiple plants of both sexes must be grown to flower stage. A ratio of two female plants to every male is recommended. Spinach is wind-pollinated, so plants grown close together will more likely achieve successful pollination; they can even be bent together and bagged with a water-resistant paper bag to aid pollination and avoid outcrossing. Seed can be dried on the stalk or in a paper bag after harvest.

SEED SAVING

Many people think the savoyed (crinkled or blistered) varieties with crumpled, blistery leaves are sweeter, although there's no denying that the smooth-leaved varieties are easier to handle in the kitchen,

TIP

and those varieties may also be more productive in the garden. Try growing one of each type and hold your own taste test.

VARIETIES

Giant Winter Its name gives it away; this is a great variety for overwintering. It produces large, medium-green, semi-savoyed leaves that stand tall even through persistent light frosts and occasional snowfalls.

Long Standing Bloomsdale The Landreth Seed Company introduced this variety in 1826, named for its company farm in Pennsylvania, and it quickly rose to prominence. It has deep green leaves that are heavily savoyed. The plant grows to 10 inches, with leaves 2 to 3 inches long and half as wide. Very prolific. Also known for its resistance to bolting.

SQUASH

Cucurbita pepo,
C. maxima,
C. moschata,
C. mixta

The squash clan comprises a truly incredible array of species and varieties, so many choices that all home gardeners should be able to find some that meet their tastes and the size of their growing area. Consider the variety of uses: sliced into salads, cooked in soups, sautéed, grilled, baked, used in pies, even simply set out in a decorative arrangement. They even can be given as "gifts"—slipped onto the porches of friends and neighbors when the zucchini production gets out of hand. And though granted its own listing in this book, the pumpkin (actually just another member of the squash family) plays a major role as Jack O'Lantern, the mascot of Halloween, in a tradition that came to us via the British in the mid-nineteenth century.

But for all the choices and potential uses, many gardeners probably return to their old favorites year after year. Indeed, that attitude is one of the bases for this book: what's been passed down to us is worth growing still. Given the space and a bit of searching, however, you can delve more deeply into the amazing world of squash by trying other varieties, new to you yet tried-and-true heirlooms.

The amazing array of choices comes from the ease of saving the squash's large seeds, but also, I think, because the fruit has captured the imagination of gardeners for so long and encouraged experimentation with cross-pollination and hybridization. However, the squash is native to North and South America, and many of the old varieties come from truly ancient lines. In Mexico, an excavated cave yielded squash seeds 9,000 years old.

There are four major species within the *Cucurbita* genus: All the summer squashes are *C. pepo,* as are pumpkins, acorn squash, spaghetti squash, and some gourds. Their plants are distinguished by pentagonal stems that have prickly spines, and they may have either bush or vining habits. Hubbard, turban, buttercup, banana, and mammoth squashes are *C. maxima* varieties, which have round stems, large leaves, and long vines. Butternut and some cushaw varieties are in *C. moschata,* characterized by pentagonal but smooth stems on large plants that thrive in hot, humid areas. Green and white cushaws are in *C. mixta*, a species only recently created as a spinoff of *C. moschata.* There are no *C. mixta* cultivars represented in this book, as most are grown in hot southern climates.

CULTIVATION

Squash require a rich soil to thrive, so mix in a generous amount of manure and compost before planting. They also require warm weather to germinate and get started, so direct-sowing in the maritime climate often produces disappointing results. Instead, plant seeds indoors in midspring, and maintain until the weather is

Early Yellow
Crookneck

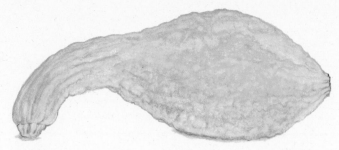

predictably warm and the garden soil is above 60°F. Young squash also have tender roots, so transplanting can sometimes do great harm. To avoid it, use peat pots or pots made of tightly wrapped newspaper, and when they're ready to go into the ground, simply plant the whole thing. Mix a complete fertilizer into the soil when planting. Make sure not to leave the lip of the peat pot above ground level. After seedlings have sprouted, thin to one plant per pot by snipping off the others at ground level rather than plucking them out, again to avoid damaging the roots.

Once the plants are in the garden, you can use a season extender like a cloche or floating row cover to keep them warmer. Maritime gardeners also use a black plastic sheet (with holes cut for the plants) as a mulch on the bed to increase heat retention and reduce weeds. The floating row cover also has the advantage of keeping off the early-season pests, such as the squash bug. Later, that pest can be destroyed by hand; it hides under leaves during the day and bores holes in the leaves at night. Its clusters of orange eggs on the undersides of leaves are a good indication of its presence. These also can be destroyed by hand.

One common mistake with squash is planting too closely. Even the smaller bush varieties need 3 to 4 feet between "hills," which are groupings of seeds or seedlings, sometimes but not always on an actual hill of soil. Larger varieties and those with long vines need even more space.

Squash require regular water and fertilizer as they grow. In the maritime climate, take care to water the base of the plant and not the leaves to avoid mildew, a common cool-season problem that shows up as a spreading whitish covering of the leaves. Water in the morning so that the plant's leaves have the entire day to dry out, because mildew takes hold in the cool, damp night air.

Squash are insect-pollinated, and varieties within the same species cross easily. You can control this by hand-pollinating (see Tip) or by growing only one plant of each species in the same garden space. Some maritime gardeners also have found that hand-pollinating increases productivity. This technique may help you get some fruit set early in the season, which is key for gaining fully mature fruits in a short-summer climate.

HARVEST AND STORAGE

Summer squash—the varieties that you use young while the fruit is small and the skin is still soft—should be harvested regularly as soon as the first fruits size up. (They may be rinsed and stored dry in the refrigerator for up to two weeks.) This will encourage more flowering, and you can get steady production from each plant. Increase the size of the winter squashes by pruning some young fruit off each vine, leaving only four or five of the best.

Rainy weather will sometimes cause the female flowers to drop off the vine. (Female flowers are distinguished by a swelling at the base of the flower that will turn into the fruit.) If that happens, harvest the male blossoms to eat; they're delicious sautéed or stuffed and baked. More flowers of each sex should blossom when the weather warms again.

Winter squash will begin to reach their stated sizes and color profiles as summer winds down. Harvest when the vines have died back, cutting off the fruits to take a bit of stem with each. Store in a cool, dry place with good ventilation. The squashes have cured when you can't dent the skin with your thumbnail. Follow instructions for each variety regarding keeping time, and check the squash supply regularly for any softening.

SEED SAVING   Harvest seed for saving by choosing the best specimen on your plant and letting it grow to full maturity. Storing it after harvest increases seed viability. After it has cured, scoop out the seeds, wash them in a colander and remove pulp, and then allow them to dry for two to three weeks on paper or a screen. Store them in an airtight jar in a cool, dark place.

TIP   Hand-pollination is the key to getting seed that will grow true to type. It's fun, and the process is not too difficult. Once flower buds start to appear, inspect the vines daily and look for viable female flowers. They will be pollinated as soon as they open, which is what you must control. The night before you expect the female flowers to open, tape or clip the blossoms shut so they can't open on their own. The next morning, visit the garden very early and pick a male flower off the plant. Strip the flower petals away to expose the pollen-covered anther, and untape the female flower. Dust the stigma at the center of the female flower with the pollen, and then reclose the flower. Mark this flower with a ribbon or cover it with a paper bag and write on it so that you know which fruit is being saved for seed.

VARIETIES OF SUMMER SQUASH

Benning's Green Tint   A productive scallop, or patty-pan, type, this variety delivers small round fruit that are white or pale green. It has a thin, waxy rind and is as early and as productive as the standard zucchini, but much more flavorful and with firmer flesh. Introduced in 1914, it was first known as Farr's White Bush for its developer, Charles N. Farr. The saucer-shaped fruits are produced on a compact bush that is great for a small garden.

Deep grooves on a long, straight, bluish green fruit distinguish this old Italian heirloom from other straight-neck summer squashes. The pronounced ribs are pale green, while the blue-green skin between them can be striped or flecked with yellow. It bruises easily, so this variety is not widely grown commercially, making it even more desirable for home growing. The flavor is rich and sweet. Its fluted shape produces scalloped medallions when it's sliced, making it attractive as well as tasty. **Costata Romanesco**

This curvaceous variety is one of the earliest cultivated in the U.S., dating from 1700. Correspondence included in *Thomas Jefferson's Garden Book* indicates that it was a native of New Jersey and was preserved by a well-known family of market gardeners there until its seed was put into circulation. It grows on a midsized bush, with the curled neck expanding to a greatly swollen blossom end. It is best eaten when less than 8 inches long and 4 inches in diameter. It has a pale yellow, mostly smooth skin when young, with whitish, dry flesh; as it ages, the color deepens and the skin can get quite covered in warts. If left to dry after they get large and warty, the fruits are also attractive as ornamental gourds. **Early Yellow Crookneck**

VARIETIES OF WINTER SQUASH

A flavorful baking squash and one of the most popular, Delicata was introduced in 1894 by the New York seed company Peter Henderson & Co. It's appropriately named, because its delicate skin makes it a short keeper, but also because the interior **Delicata** flesh—once you get beyond the numerous seeds in its long center cavity—is quite a delicacy. The flesh is orange, dry, and quite sweet; the edible skin can range from a creamy pale green to medium green with yellow or orange, with long stripes of dark green and often blotches or stripes of orange or yellow. The leaves of this *C. pepo* variety are silvery green and smaller than those of most squashes, on a 10-foot vine that can be trellised. For the urban gardener, this compact size is a blessing, because each plant can produce a number of 2- to 3-pound squash, which average 8 inches long and 3 inches in diameter.

Hubbard   With a shape more like a football than a fruit, the Hubbard is a distinctive specimen. It is also one of America's most treasured squashes. From the *C. maxima* species, its cultivation is traced to the port town of Marblehead, Massachusetts, where Mrs. Elizabeth Hubbard passed seeds of the variety on to the local seed company of J.J.H. Gregory. She told Gregory that the seeds had come to her from a local sea captain, and he named the variety after her when introducing it in his catalog in about 1850. The Hubbard's extremely hard, sometimes bumpy shell makes it a great keeper—and a major challenge to cut through. Inside is a rich golden-yellow flesh that is dry, sweet, and dense. Its unique oval shape—tapering to a point on one or both ends—can today be found in dusty blue or gold, as well as green, the color of the original strain. Fruits can be quite large, to 15 pounds.

Marina di Chioggia   This large, deep-green squash will surely amaze visitors who see it lurking beneath its huge leaves. Marina's origin is South America, but it gets its name from the famed Italian coastal town of Chioggia, where it was also called "sea pumpkin." A Hubbard-style member of the *C. maxima* species, it is unusual and stunning; the slightly flattened sphere is covered in warts and bumps and dark vertical grooves. It grows to 10 pounds on a large vine that may produce five to six fruits. Cut it for roasting, and you find rich yellow flesh around a hollow center. Sweet and flavorful, it is also great for pie.

Also known as Hokkaido, this teardrop-shaped variety is bright reddish orange and produces a number of 4- to 6-pound fruits on a typically large *C. maxima* vine. It has meaty golden flesh that is dry and sweet, and it keeps well.

Red Kuri

One of the handiest squashes for single use, this *C. pepo* variety is prized for baking and stuffing; a 1- to 2-pound squash, cut in half, can perfectly serve two people. Along with that convenience, it has a rich-tasting yellow flesh that is firm, sweet, and slightly nutty. You can just detect a shade of green on its nearly black skin, a 6-inch ovoid with deep vertical fluting. Its shell is hard enough to allow longer post-harvest storage than many squash. Possibly of Native American origin with the Arikara people of the Plains states, this variety was introduced to the seed trade by the Iowa Seed Co. in 1913.

Table Queen Acorn

An American favorite that's not quite as old as many heirlooms, dating only from 1944, it has won a place at the table because of its reliable production as well as its thick golden flesh. The exterior is tan, and the squash is shaped like a broad-necked bottle. A member of the *C. moschata* species, it produces vines that are not as overpowering as those of some varieties, allowing each plant's four to five fruits to come to maturity earlier—a bonus in the maritime climate's shorter warm season. The sweet, nutty fruit has a relatively small seed cache and grows to 5 pounds. It keeps quite well into the winter.

Waltham Butternut

TOMATILLO & GROUND CHERRY

Physalis ixocarpa and P. pruinosa

Many a "salsa garden" contains the unique tomatillo. These are the firm, husk-covered fruits that have some characteristics of a tomato, but with a tangy, fresh taste that leans more toward a tart apple crossed with a sweet pepper. Tomatillos (*P. ixocarpa*), and their cousins the ground cherries (*P. pruinosa*, which is more of a dessert or jam fruit than a salsa ingredient), are wonderfully easy plants to have in your garden, and they provide visual interest as well as unique flavors.

The visual part comes with the husk, which is actually the plant's calyx—the group of sepals that form the outer petals of a flower. In the tomatillo and ground-cherry genus, the calyx continues to grow into a bulb-shaped, papery layer that covers the fruit until it is ripe. Fully formed, it looks like the shell of the Chinese lantern flower, which many people recognize from flower arrangements.

Growing in your garden, this fruit will attract attention, but not just for its pendulous paper lanterns; the plant itself ranges across the ground and is prolifically covered with flowers that are a favorite of bees. The tomatillo plant can grow as high as 3 feet and spreads its branches out to easily cover 3 to 4 feet in rangy, open form, so it must be given space. Its growth habit is something like that of a nonclinging vine. Leaves are heart-shaped and poisonous; flowers are small, triangular, and bright yellow. The ground cherry is lower-growing if not more compact; it barely rises above the soil and branches out thickly with dense leaf growth in the manner of a groundcover.

The flesh of these fruits is firm and crisp, but with the contained juiciness of a cucumber. Tomatillos can be rather tart and tangy, while ground cherries tend to be sweet. As they grow inside their husks, both are green and very hard, but maturity will soften them and their ultimate color will appear. Tomatillos are purple, tan, or green, and ground cherries are yellow or orange. Another big difference: tomatillos can grow to golf-ball size, while ground cherries are more in the marble category—making harvesting and processing them for use a fairly tedious chore.

Largely grown like tomatoes, tomatillos and ground cherries require little care once established. They can be started from seed, indoors or *in situ,* or can be purchased as starts. They like a fertilized, loose soil with good drainage, but will perform under many conditions. Space

CULTIVATION

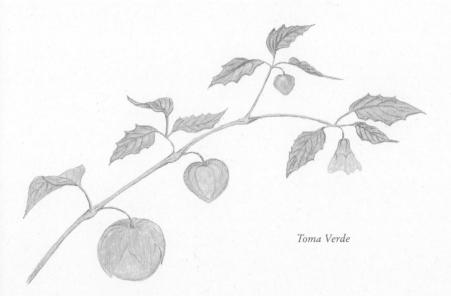

Toma Verde

the plants generously, maybe 3 feet apart, perhaps allowing them to hang over the edges of walls or raised beds. Mulch around the base will help retain moisture and reduce weeds, and a balanced fertilizer applied at the beginning of flowering can boost production.

HARVEST AND STORAGE   Both tomatillos and ground cherries will tell you when it's harvest time: fruits, full in their husks, will begin to be released from the plant and drop to the ground. At this time, the husks are drying or completely dry and brittle and have split open to reveal the fruits. If some drop, feel the husks of others to determine if they're full and softening. The fruits will be slightly sticky and so should be harvested promptly to avoid attracting insects. Remove husks and rinse off the stickiness before using.

Also, look for the proper color of the varieties you're growing, as eating the unripe fruit is inadvisable; it reportedly makes some people sick. If you must remove the plant from the garden before the fruit is totally ripe, pull it and hang it upside down in a dry place. The fruits can be refrigerated in their husks for up to two weeks, but may rot if stored when wet.

SEED SAVING   Seed is saved in the same manner as pepper and tomato seeds. Scoop the plentiful seeds out of the center of a desirable specimen and immerse in a jar of water. Leave them to ferment for a few days, scooping the scum off and changing the water a couple of times. The good seeds will sink to the bottom and, once captured in a fine strainer and rinsed, they can be laid on a paper plate in a single layer to dry. When thoroughly dry, store them in a paper sleeve, inside an airtight container.

TIP   Friends who have grown ground cherries and tomatillos might be a good source for seeds or starts if you can't find these in the catalogs; both species seed freely into the garden and often send up volunteers the following season, which are easily transplanted.

VARIETIES

A Polish variety that has been grown in the U.S. since at least 1837, this prolific plant produces sweet, half-inch-diameter berries that are golden when ripe, inside a honey-brown husk. The plant has a dense, spreading habit with grey-green, vinelike leaves.

Aunt Molly's ground cherry

The familiar green tomatillo of many gardens, also known as the husk tomato, comes most likely from Central America, and was known to be a food of the Aztecs, although evidence of the plant has been found much earlier, before the year AD 900. It has become popular and widely cultivated in Mexico. Its seedy fruit, which can grow to more than 2 inches in diameter, is the key ingredient in green salsa, adding an acidic, somewhat citrusy flavor. It is also wonderful sliced and smeared with goat cheese. When it's sautéed, a sweet, nutty flavor will develop.

Toma Verde tomatillo

TOMATO

Lycopersicon lycopersicum

Certainly no homegrown vegetable is more in demand than the tomato. A just-off-the-vine tomato is prized for its flavor, juiciness, and freshness, and growing your own rather than simply buying whatever happens to be available has become a badge of honor for the home gardener.

As a symbol, too, the tomato is hard to beat. The vining plant yearns for the sun and enthusiastically sends out shoots once it's taken hold in the soil. The sun is reflected back in the tomato's small, soft-yellow flowers, from whose modest size can spring anything from a sweet little gumball-sized cherry tomato all the way up to a multilobed, full-sized slicer whose weight is gauged in pounds, but might as well be measured in gold. The fruit, in all its varieties, reflects also the richness of the summer growing season. It is hard to watch the ripening of the first tomato without feeling that life is good.

The tomato's history is almost as rich as its flavor. Born in the mountain ranges of Central and South America, it grew into use by native peoples over thousands of years, eventually migrating north into Mexico. There, in 1519, the Spanish invader Cortéz and his conquistadors discovered the plant and took it back to Spain. It was quickly adopted both there and in Italy, and then made its way to U.S. There is evidence early colonists grew it, but the written record of it in this country began when Thomas Jefferson recorded it as one of his plants in his garden book in 1781.

It did not catch on widely until early in the nineteenth century, adoption being slowed by rumors of its being poisonous or causing cancer. Once put on the table, though, its popularity skyrocketed, and the styles, sizes, colors, and shapes of tomatoes began to multiply. Today, there are literally thousands of varieties in circulation among seed-savers, although the number offered commercially is considerably fewer, perhaps a hundred. Heirloom varieties have recently seen a resurgence, and the trend of losing varieties to near extinction is being reversed in a small way. Seed companies are seeking the old tomatoes from seed banks and private growers, and putting some of the old varieties back into circulation when they find ones that grow well.

Flavor is the prime factor for the home gardener, which is at its height when fresh picked. But that has been sacrificed by the commercial grower in favor of shelf stability and hardiness for travel. As most tomato lovers know, selecting varieties for those supermarket traits can work against the fresh-and-flavorful goal.

Tomatoes like as much sun as you can give them. Choose a spot that gets at least six hours of full sun; against a warm stone wall or fence is a bonus. The soil should be well composted for moisture retention. To reduce the incidence of soil-borne disease, rotate tomatoes into different beds each year if possible. Prepare the bed with an organic fertilizer high in phosphorus and potassium but not too rich in nitrogen.

In the maritime climate, it is wise to start tomatoes in flats and continue to size them up in pots, waiting to plant them until the ground and the weather has warmed. The soil temperature should be at least 60°F.

For my Seattle garden, I sow the seeds in March, placing the seed flats on a surface heated from below. Once the plants are up, bottom heat is not needed, but extra light is helpful. Transplant to 2-inch pots when the starts have grown their third set of leaves, and to 4-inch pots when the plants are 4 inches tall. When they've reached twice that height, transplant again, into gallon-size pots. Each time I pot them up, and also when planting them out, I set the root ball deep into the hole so part of the plant's stem is beneath

CULTIVATION

Brandywine

the new soil surface, first pinching off leaves that will be below soil level. This helps strengthen the plant, because advantageous rooting will occur, with new roots sprouting from the fine hairs along its stem.

Space determinate varieties 18 to 24 inches apart, and indeterminate ones 2 to 3 feet apart. (Determinate tomatoes send up one central stalk to a certain height, then set their fruit, which will mostly come ripe at once. This is the type favored by commercial growers and is also best for growing in pots on the patio. Indeterminate plants, as most heirlooms are, have a much more pronounced vining habit, and will continue to grow and set fruit throughout the season.) The two types have different support needs as well: a determinate variety will be happy if tied to a single stake set close to its main stem, while an indeterminate one needs a broader support, such as a trellis or cage, to hold its stems and its heavier fruit supply.

A sturdy bamboo trellis or heavy-gauge metal grid is preferable to the flimsy circular wire cages that are inexplicably popular. Hog wire, used for fencing swine, works quite well, as it can either be attached to strong posts and used as a tall, straight trellis or formed into a circle and staked to make a cage. If you're growing tomatoes against a fence, you can use a web of heavy twine attached to the fence.

As the tomatoes grow, loosely tie their main stems to the trellis. For indeterminate varieties, I often allow three or four main stems to develop, and prune off extras. More space will allow sun to get to the fruit for better ripening. It also will help air circulate through the plants, essential to avoiding the fungal disease late blight, a very common maritime tomato ailment because it thrives on continually damp leaves. Avoid overhead watering, and use a straw mulch on the soil to further reduce the chance of splash-borne late blight.

Keep the plants evenly watered while developing, and side-dress with additional fertilizer as they begin to flower. When the fruits have all set and are beginning to ripen, cut back or discontinue watering to hasten the ripening process. If they are ripening very late in the season, begin to cut back the leafy growth to expose more of them to the sun.

After harvest, remove tomato plants promptly from the garden to minimize late blight, which will live in the soil. To be safe, send all tomato plants off to a commercial yard-waste composting; backyard compost bins will generally not get hot enough to kill the fungus.

HARVEST AND STORAGE

Pick slicing tomatoes and salad tomatoes when the color deepens and the tomatoes begin to feel heavy. The skin should yield slightly to pressure and not be completely firm. Cherry tomatoes can be picked as the color brightens and by taste. Paste tomatoes need to be fully red, heavy, and more yielding to pressure.

Ripe tomatoes should be eaten immediately upon picking. They will store on the kitchen counter (never store them in the refrigerator) for a few days, depending upon ripeness.

When harvesting partially ripe tomatoes at the end of the season, place them in a single layer in a paper bag, then close the top to keep it dark. Most tomatoes will ripen in this way, but will be less flavorful.

SEED SAVING

Scoop the pulp from the center of a desirable specimen and immerse in a jar of water. Stir well to loosen the seeds from the pulp. The mixture will ferment, with scum and immature seeds rising to the surface. Skim that off and change the water until the fermentation clears and only good seeds remain on the bottom. Strain off the water and spread the seeds in a single layer on paper to dry. When thoroughly dry, store in a paper sleeve, inside an airtight container. Mark the variety and date the package.

TIP   After the plants have gained some height and begun to branch out, pinch off most of the sucker shoots that sprout from the V-shaped intersections of the main stem and the branches. This concentrates the plant's energy into a strong branching system that will supply and support a good crop of fruit, allows good air circulation, and provides plenty of light.

VARIETIES OF SLICERS

Amish Paste   Originating with the Amish people in Wisconsin, this variety produces large oxheart-shaped tomatoes on a vigorous indeterminate vine. The fruit, which has won taste tests in the U.S. and Australia, is dark red, full of flavor, solid, and less seedy than many varieties. Despite its name, it can be eaten fresh as well as used in sauce.

Black Krim   "Splendid Table" chef and cookbook author Lynne Rossetto Kasper says this variety has "incredible complexity and depth," likening it to "an aged Bordeaux; deep and meaty." The large, mottled, reddish brown fruit with green shoulders has a hint of saltiness that reminds you of its Black Sea origins. It is juicy, sweet, and often a taste-test winner. Grows on a medium-sized, indeterminate plant.

Brandywine   The granddaddy of heirloom tomatoes, Brandywine is a large beefsteak variety grown throughout the U.S. It is not a sure bet for maritime climates because it needs a fairly long season to develop and the fruit comes on late. However, it's worth a try, based on your light and heat conditions, because its flavor is prized. The large, slightly flattened globes with blossom-end crevices are juicy and mildly acidic, with a strong tomato flavor throughout. Standard Brandywines are pink, but there is a red strain, and a yellow one that ripens to a rich gold. Because the skins are thin, this tomato does not pack or ship well, so it will rarely be seen in the markets—making it all the more appealing for home growing.

Cherokee Purple

Said to have been grown by the Cherokee Indians, who gave seeds to a Tennessee grower more than one hundred years ago, this variety produces medium-sized round fruit, ripening in a short enough growing season to suit many conditions. Like many other darker-hued varieties, it has a dusky, winey flavor, and it is quite sweet. The reddish purple fruits have green streaks across their shoulders, with the purple and green bleeding into the firm, solid flesh.

Costoluto Genovese

A heavily lobed, flattened globe, this variety is as unique as its name. Its color is dark red with a blush of orange around the stem. The lobes are separated by deep grooves, making the fruit resemble a billowy accordion. Originating on the Italian Riviera, it thrives in a hot summer, rewarding growers with a rich, juicy, complex taste.

Green Zebra

Of all the tomatoes that are green when ripe, this one is the star. The fruit starts off dark green with lime-green stripes, but as it matures, the dark background turns a minty yellow and the stripes a deeper green. The abundant fruits are not large, perhaps 2 inches across, but they have a bold flavor both acidic and sweet. Green Zebra was developed from other heirlooms by master plant breeder Tom Wagner of Everett, Washington.

Mortgage Lifter

A sturdy beefsteak with a blue-collar pedigree, this variety gives you a great story as well as a meaty, mild flavor. Also known as Radiator Charlie's Mortgage Lifter, it was developed in the 1930s by radiator repairman M. C. "Charlie" Byles of Logan, West

Virginia. He cross-pollinated four beefsteak varieties year after year, putting the biggest one in the center of his patch and surrounding it by the others. After seven years, he came up with this variety, and began selling plants for one dollar each. With six years of proceeds, he paid off his $6,000 home mortgage. The large wine-red fruits, which may crack along the shoulders, grow on a vigorous indeterminate plant.

Mr. Stripey   Also sold as Tigerella, this smaller striped tomato originated as an English greenhouse variety. Fruits are 2 inches across, bright red with orange stripes. It has a full-flavored, tangy taste. Indeterminate vines produce fruit fairly early and predictably in cooler climates.

Silvery Fir Tree   Fernlike foliage forms a beautiful grey-green haze around the fruit on this compact, determinate plant that originated in the former Soviet Union. Fruit is red, solid and slightly flattened globes of 2 to 3 inches. Quite prolific, and a great plant for pot or patio growing. A midseason variety, it will do well in climates with shorter summers.

VARIETIES OF CHERRY TOMATOES

Chadwick's   A large cherry that was developed by the renowned English horticulturalist Alan Chadwick, who brought the concepts of biodynamic growing to the U.S. through a teaching position at the University of California at Santa Cruz. Vigorous indeterminate vines produce scores of large, round cherries, sweet, meaty, and flavorful.

Red Fig   One of the few tomatoes described by Fearing Burr Jr. in his 1863 *The Field and Garden Vegetables of America*, this "fig" type (akin to the pear tomato) produces small, deep-red fruits that may grow to a teardrop or pear shape. Fruit is mild and less firm than some. Good for drying or canning, it was very popular for making "tomato figs" in Burr's day, which were soaked in syrup and then dried. Plants can be susceptible to late blight and are less productive than some varieties.

A delectable, stunning variety that is the prize of farmers markets and home gardeners alike, Yellow Pear delivers tons of large, deep-yellow fruits with narrow necks flaring out to generous globes an inch across. This variety dates back at least to the early 1800s, and possibly much earlier. Decorative in salads, and great for a refreshing snack while you're working in the garden.

Yellow Pear

BIBLIOGRAPHY
BOOKS ABOUT HEIRLOOM VEGETABLES AND HISTORICAL GARDENING

Adams, Denise Wiles. *Restoring American Gardens: An Encyclopedia of Heirloom Ornamental Plants, 1640-1940*. Portland, OR: Timber Press, 2004.

Ausubel, Kenny. *Seeds of Change: The Living Treasure*. San Francisco: Harper SF, 1994.

Baron, Robert C., ed. *The Garden and Farm Books of Thomas Jefferson*. Golden, CO: Fulcrum, 1987.

Bender, Steve, and Felder Rushing. *Passalong Plants*. Chapel Hill, NC: University of North Carolina Press, 1993.

Buist, Robert. *The Family Kitchen Gardener*. New York: C. M. Saxton, 1853 (out of print).

Burr Jr., Fearing. *The Field and Garden Vegetables of America*, 3d ed. Chillicothe, IL: The American Botanist Booksellers, 1988 (first published by J. E. Tilton & Co., Boston, 1863).

Cobbett, William. *The American Gardener*. New York: The Modern Library, 2003 (first published in London, 1821).

Coulter, Lynn. *Gardening with Heirloom Seeds*. Chapel Hill, NC: University of North Carolina Press, 2006.

Creasy, Rosalind. *The Edible Heirloom Garden*. Boston: Periplus Editions, 1999.

Goldman, Amy. *The Compleat Squash: A Passionate Grower's Guide to Pumpkins, Squashes, and Gourds*. New York: Artisan, 2004.

——. *The Heirloom Tomato: From Garden to Table: Recipes, Portraits, and History of the World's Most Beautiful Fruit*. New York: Bloomsbury USA, 2008.

Jabs, Carolyn. *The Heirloom Gardener*. San Francisco: Sierra Club Books, 1984.

Larkcom, Joy. *Oriental Vegetables: The Complete Guide for the Gardening Cook*. New York: Kodansha America, 2007.

Luebbermann, Mimi. *Heirloom Gardens: Simple Secrets for Old-Fashioned Flowers and Vegetables*. San Francisco: Chronicle Books, 1997.

Male, Carolyn. *100 Heirloom Tomatoes for the American Garden*. New York: Workman, 1999.

McMahon, Bernard. *The American Gardener's Calendar*. Whitefish, MT: Kessinger Publishing, 2007 (first published by B. Graves, Philadelphia, 1806).

Vilmorin-Andrieux, MM. *The Vegetable Garden: Illustrations, Descriptions, and Culture of the Garden Vegetables of Cold and Temperate Climates*, translated by W. Miller. Berkeley, CA: Ten Speed Press, 1981 (reprint of 1885 edition).

Viola, Herman J., and Carolyn Margolis, eds. *Seeds of Change: A Quincentennial Celebration*. Washington, D.C.: Smithsonian Institution Press, 1991.

Warner, Charles Dudley. *My Summer in a Garden*. New York: Modern Library, 2002 (first published in 1870).

Watson, Benjamin. *Taylor's Guide to Heirloom Vegetables*. New York: Houghton Mifflin, 1996.

Weaver, William Woys. *100 Vegetables and Where They Came From*. Chapel Hill, NC: Algonquin, 2000.

——. *Heirloom Vegetable Gardening: A Master Gardener's Guide to Planting, Seed Saving, and Cultural History*. New York: Henry Holt, 1999.

Welch, William C., and Greg Grant. *The Southern Heirloom Garden*. Dallas, TX: Taylor, 1995.

Whealy, Kent, et al. *Seed Savers Exchange: The First 10 Years*. Decorah, IA: Seed Savers Publications, 1986.

White, Lyman. *Heirlooms and Genetics: 100 Years of Seeds*. Cambridge, NY: self-published, 1988.

Yepsen, Roger. *A Celebration of Heirloom Vegetables: Growing and Cooking Old-Time Varieties*. New York: Artisan, 1998.

Books About
Maritime Gardening

Colebrook, Binda. *Winter Gardening in the Maritime Northwest.* Seattle: Sasquatch Books, 1998.

Head, William. *Gardening Under Cover: A Northwest Guide to Solar Greenhouses, Cold Frames, and Cloches.* Seattle: Sasquatch Books, 1989.

Seattle Tilth Association. *The Maritime Northwest Garden Guide,* rev. ed. Seattle, 2007.

Solomon, Steve. *Growing Vegetables West of the Cascades,* 6th ed. Seattle: Sasquatch Books, 2007.

Resources
Seed Companies

Any seed company that offers heirlooms will address some or all of the following concepts:

Open-pollinated seeds – "OP" plants are those whose seed will grow back true in the next season. Saving seed from these plants is a valuable way for gardeners to save money, reduce their carbon footprint, and become more self-sufficient.

Organic seed – Gardeners who want to grow the healthiest food in the manner least harmful to nature often choose organic seed. If the seed company has decided against organic certification, it still might be committed to nontoxic gardening and farming practices.

Untreated seed – Many seed companies will treat their seed with pesticides or chemicals, but companies offering heirlooms typically sell untreated seed. This means it might require more care on the gardener's part when planting (not too early, for instance) to ensure successful germination.

Family-owned or nonprofit – Many seed companies committed to heirlooms are independent firms rather than subsidiaries of a large corporation, or are operated by nonprofit organizations committed to, in the words of Seed Savers Exchange, "preserving our vegetable heritage." Some, like SSE, even operate seed banks, working to ensure that old varieties do not get lost.

Bio-regional – Some seed companies will focus on seeds that grow well in a particular region. **Companies with a particular connection to maritime or short-season climates are marked with an asterisk.**

Safe Seed Pledge – Many companies dedicated to these concepts have signed a "Safe Seed Pledge" and will link to it on their websites. The pledge was created by the Council for Responsible Genetics and says, in part, "We pledge that we do not knowingly buy or sell genetically engineered seeds or plants." For more information, see www.gene-watch.org.

U.S. SEED COMPANIES

*Abundant Life Seeds, Cottage Grove, OR, www.abundantlifeseeds.com
This catalog focuses on organically grown rare and endangered seeds, and includes many heirlooms. It is owned by the same family that operates Territorial Seed Company.

Baker Creek Heirloom Seeds, Mansfield, MO, www.rareseeds.com
Enthusiastic heirloom promoters offer a comprehensive listing of heirloom seeds. The company also publishes The Heirloom Gardener magazine and hosts annual festivals.

Botanical Interests, Broomfield, CO, www.botanicalinterests.com
Online catalog includes special section of heirlooms.

Bountiful Gardens, Willits, CA, www.bountifulgardens.org
Exclusively heirloom and open-pollinated varieties. A project of Ecology Action, the research and education organization founded by John Jeavons.

Evergreen Seeds, Anaheim, CA, www.evergreenseeds.com
Extensive collection of Asian vegetable seeds.

*Fedco Seed Co., Waterville, ME,
www.fedcoseeds.com
Specializing in cold-hardy varieties. The company is
organized as a cooperative.

*Filaree Farm, Okanogan, WA,
www.filareefarm.com
Selling the widest variety of seed garlic available.

*Garlicsmiths, Kettle Falls, WA,
www.garlicsmiths.com
Selling a wide variety of seed garlic.

*Good Seed Company, Oroville, WA,
www.goodseedco.net
Heirloom seeds especially adapted for the northern
garden, grown two miles from the Canadian border in
northcentral Washington.

Heirloom Seeds, West Elizabeth, PA,
www.heirloomseeds.com
A family-owned seed business specializing in
heirlooms.

*Irish Eyes Garden Seeds, Ellensburg, WA,
www.gardencityseeds.net
Offering an extensive collection of certified
Washington seed potatoes as well as other seed
and supplies.

J.L. Hudson, Seedsman, La Honda, CA,
www.jlhudsonseeds.net
A public-access seed bank, established in 1911, with
heirloom vegetables among a much larger seed catalog.

*Johnny's Selected Seeds, Winslow, ME,
www.johnnyseeds.com
An employee-owned company with an extensive seed
catalog and many heirlooms.

*Kitazawa Seed Company, Oakland, CA,
www.kitazawaseed.com
A family-owned company specializing in high-quality
Asian vegetable seeds.

D. Landreth Seed Company, Baltimore, MD,
www.landrethseeds.com
Heirloom and classic seeds from the oldest seed house
in the United States, begun in 1784.

Native Seeds/SEARCH, Tucson, AZ,
www.nativeseeds.org
Catalog contains an extensive list of corn, beans,
peppers (listed under "chile") and other heat-loving
crops. This nonprofit conservation organization
conserves seed from the Southwestern United States
and northeastern Mexico.

The Natural Gardening Company, Petaluma, CA,
www.naturalgardening.com
Extensive catalog, with many heirloom, open-
pollinated, and organic seeds from the first
certified-organic nursery in the United States.

*Nichols Garden Nursery, Albany, OR,
www.nicholsgardennursery.com
Rare and unusual seeds, many of them heirlooms,
come from this Willamette Valley nursery that is
more than fifty years old.

*Peters Seed & Research, Myrtle Creek, OR,
www.psrseed.com
A small seed company that emphasizes research and
breeding but also carries many heirloom varieties.

Redwood City Seed Company, Redwood City, CA,
www.ecoseeds.com
Focus is on a wide variety of peppers, but this
company also offers a selection of other heirloom
vegetables.

Renee's Garden, Felton, CA,
www.reneesgarden.com
Heirlooms are among the many varieties chosen by
Renee Shepherd, who previously owned Shepherd's
Garden Seeds.

Ronniger Potato Farm, Austin, CO,
www.ronnigers.com
This company has an extensive catalog of certified
Colorado seed potatoes, including many heirloom
varieties. Also sells garlic.

Seed Savers Exchange, Decorah, IA,
www.seedsavers.org
The largest nongovernmental seed bank in the
United States, this nonprofit organization also offers
an extensive catalog of seeds preserved by them, as
well as a seed-exchange program for members that
annually lists thousands of varieties, many unavailable
commercially.

Seeds of Change, Santa Fe, NM,
www.seedsofchange.com
Its extensive catalog of organic vegetable and flower
seed includes a collection of heirlooms.

Southern Exposure Seed Exchange, Mineral, VA,
www.southernexposure.com
Located near Thomas Jefferson's historic home,
Monticello, this company focuses on heirloom seeds
that grow well in the mid-Atlantic region, but sells to
gardeners throughout the United States.

*Territorial Seed Company, Cottage Grove, OR,
www.territorial-seeds.com
The premier bio-regional seed company for the Pacific
Northwest, with an extensive catalog that includes
many heirloom varieties.

*Victory Seed Company, Molalla, OR,
www.victoryseeds.com
Rare, open-pollinated and heirloom seeds, some grown
on the company's own farm.

*Wild Garden Seed, Philomath, OR,
www.wildgardenseed.com
All seed from this company is grown at Gathering
Together Farm in northcentral Oregon.

CANADIAN SEED COMPANIES
Because of customs regulations, these firms
will ship seeds only to Canada.

Boundary Garlic Farm, Midway, BC,
www.garlicfarm.ca
Family-owned firm selling heritage seed garlic.

The Cottage Gardener, Newtonville, ON,
www.cottagegardener.com
Southern Ontario seed house and nursery selling
organic heirloom seeds.

Salt Spring Seeds, Salt Spring Island, BC,
www.saltspringseeds.com
Focused on heirlooms and heritage vegetable seed.
The company also created the Seed and Plant
Sanctuary, which is a gene bank and seed collection
of plants that grow well in Canada.

Seeds of Victoria, Victoria, BC,
www.earthfuture.com/gardenpath
Operated by the nonprofit Garden Path Centre;
includes some heirlooms.

Stellar Seeds, Sorrento, BC,
www.stellarseeds.com
Organic vegetable, herb, and flower seeds,
including many heirloom varieties.

West Coast Seeds, Vancouver, BC,
www.westcoastseeds.com
Carries an extensive catalog that includes many
heirlooms.

SEED SAVERS NETWORKS

Arche Noah, Schiltern, Austria,
www.arche-noah.at/etomite/
The organization houses one of Europe's largest seed
banks, has a seed-savers network and an organic
demonstration garden, hosts events, and provides
education and political involvement on plant genetic
issues.

Henry Doubleday Research Association,
Warwickshire, UK,
www.gardenorganic.org.uk/
Garden Organic is the working name for the HDRA,
which has been promoting organic gardening and
sustainability for more than fifty years. Its Heritage
Seed Library maintains a collection of mainly
European varieties that are no longer commercially
available; its members, called Seed Guardians, also
share hundreds of varieties.

Native Seeds/SEARCH, Tucson, AZ,
www.nativeseeds.org
This organization, the Southwestern Endangered
Aridlands Resource Clearing House, conserves seed
from the Southwestern United States and northeastern
Mexico. In addition to its seed bank, it offers seeds
for sale. It is part of a coalition promoting the RAFT
(Renewing America's Food Traditions) Initiative,
which documents, celebrates, and safeguards the
unique foods of North America.

Seed Savers Exchange, Decorah, IA,
www.seedsavers.org
SSE maintains the largest nongovernmental seed
bank in the United States on its northern Iowa farm,
offers an extensive seed catalog, and operates a seed
exchange program for members that annually lists
thousands of varieties, many unavailable commercially.
The nonprofit published the excellent resource
and bestselling book *Seed to Seed: Seed Saving and
Growing Techniques for Vegetable Gardeners,* by
Suzanne Ashworth.

Seed Savers Network, Byron Bay, New South Wales,
Australia, www.seedsavers.net
Organized in 1986, this nonprofit maintains a seed
bank, has produced a widely sold handbook on seed
saving, and has helped start seed-saving organizations
in other countries.

Seeds of Diversity, Toronto, Ontario, Canada,
www.seeds.ca

Canada's heritage seed program for gardeners, this
nonprofit facilitates seed sharing by members, and
provides education on horticultural heritage and
preserving food biodiversity. It also maintains a
heritage plants database and hosts events across the
country.

The Thomas Jefferson Center for Historic Plants,
Charlottesville, VA, www.monticello.org
The gardens at Monticello have been restored and are
maintained with the plants and techniques used by
the third U.S. president. This organization maintains
heritage gardens, produces research, and offers some
plants and seeds for sale.

COMMUNITY GARDENING

In any major city (and many smaller ones) in the
maritime Northwest, people without land of their
own can get involved in community gardening. Often
the gardens will be on city-owned or leased land, and
the gardeners pay a small yearly fee. These gardens
are great places to meet people and learn more about
gardening, and they are a valuable link to provide local
food security, as they often have "giving gardens"
grown for food-bank customers.

American Community Gardening Association,
www.communitygarden.org

Community Gardens, City of Vancouver, BC, Canada,
www.city.vancouver.bc.ca/parks/parks/comgardn.htm

Community Gardens, Portland, OR,
www.portlandonline.com/parks/index.cfm?c=39846

Community Gardens, San Francisco, CA,
www.parks.sfgov.org/site/recpark_index.asp?id=27048

City Farmer, Vancouver, BC, Canada,
www.cityfarmer.info/

P-Patch Program, City of Seattle, www.seattle.gov
/Neighborhoods/ppatch/